# THE
# HUNGRY
# STUDENT
# COOKBOOK

## 200+
### QUICK AND SIMPLE RECIPES

spruce

An Hachette UK Company
www.hachette.co.uk

First published in Great Britain in 2013 by Spruce
a division of Octopus Publishing Group Ltd
Endeavour House, 189 Shaftesbury Avenue
London, WC2H 8JY
www.octopusbooks.co.uk

ISBN 978-1-84601-418-5

A CIP catalogue record for this book is available
from the British Library

Printed and bound in China

10 9 8 7 6 5 4 3 2

Drinking excessive alcohol can significantly
damage your health. The UK Health Department
recommends men do not regularly exceed 3–4
units a day and women 2–3 units. Never operate
a vehicle when you have been drinking alcohol.
Octopus Publishing Group accepts no liability
or responsibility for any consequences resulting
from the use of or reliance upon the information
contained herein.

This book includes dishes made with nuts and
nut derivatives.

Do not mix metric and imperial measurements.

Standard level spoon measurements are used in
all recipes.
1 tablespoon = one 15 ml spoon
1 teaspoon = one 5 ml spoon

Ovens should be preheated to the specified
temperature – if using a fan-assisted oven, follow
the manufacturer's instructions for adjusting the
time and the temperature.

Some of the recipes in this book have been
previously published by Hamlyn.

# CONTENTS

# INTRODUCTION

You have secured your place on a course, and you have found somewhere to live, and now all that's left to do is pack your bags. Leaving home for the first time is one of the biggest events in anyone's life and, although your folks will probably be on hand to bail you out when you lose your wallet and greet you with open arms when you head home with a sack of dirty washing, you're still taking that first independent leap into the unknown, with all the excitement, uncertainty and hangovers that it involves.

Whether you're moving into halls or shared housing, you're going to have to start looking after yourself. If you're used to your meals miraculously appearing from the kitchen every night and your clothes being laundered and neatly folded on your bed, this could come as a bit of a shock. It's time to become familiar with household appliances and to learn how to use them without flooding or burning down your digs. And there's no excuse: if you can download apps on to a smartphone, you can almost certainly locate and manipulate the controls on a washing machine so that you have some clean undergarments.

## SPACE INVADERS

You may or may not be studying politics, but you're likely to have to use some skills of diplomacy and negotiation when you move in with your housemates. If you're sharing with a bunch of people you don't know – and now have to share a bathroom and kitchen with – then it's going to take a while to set some ground rules so that you can live harmoniously together under one roof.

When it comes to cleaning, one student's den of iniquity is another's homage to cleanliness, and whether you get on with your housemates in the pub is irrelevant when you're faced with a sink full of pasta-encrusted plates and mugs you could donate to medical science. A cleaning rota might sound like a draconian option when you're embarking on a few years of living by your own rules, but it's a good way to name and shame the soap-dodgers and to stop your house from descending into total chaos. When it comes to the point where the only living creatures that want to visit the kitchen are rodents, you will appreciate the benefits of a rota.

## FINDER'S KEEPERS

Different people have different views on food rights. While you might firmly believe that your precious piece of mature Cheddar should be left untouched for when you have a sudden cheese craving, your housemates might have more socialist leanings and believe that all food is up for grabs. Again, you need to decide on an agreed protocol on moving-in day: will all food be fair game, or are you going to allocate refrigerator and cupboard space to each housemate and hold a public enquiry if so much as a square of chocolate is unaccounted for?

If you're living with more than a couple of people, it isn't practicable to traipse off to the supermarket together on a weekly basis. Apart from looking like a bedraggled version of the Von Trapp family huddled around a communal shopping trolley, the discussions over ingredients, likes and dislikes and special offers will eat substantially into your study or social time. It's far better to nominate a 'shopper' each week and agree on a basic shopping list for the items that everyone will use (condiments, loo roll, beans, pasta, bread, milk and so on). If someone has a penchant for duck liver pâté – or something else that doesn't come under the 'essentials' label – they can buy and enjoy it separately.

## DIRTY FILM

We're talking now about the film of scum on your work surfaces, which will soon build up if you don't occasionally run a cloth around your kitchen. It won't take too many late-night food binges or missed ticks on the cleaning rota for your kitchen to degenerate into something squatters would run a mile from. The longer you leave it, the more difficult it will be to clean, and there's a greater likelihood that the area will become a breeding ground for flies, maggots and curious furry friends.

Here are ten simple tips to help you avoid a trip to hospital.
- Keep food covered so it's protected from pesky flies.
- Keep raw meat covered and on the lowest shelf in the refrigerator, away from other food to prevent contamination.
- Wash your hands before you start preparing food – you might be immune to your own germs, but your housemates won't be.
- Wash fruit and vegetables before you prepare them. Remember that quite a few people will have handled the fruit and veg before they arrive in your kitchen.
- Use scorching hot water for washing up and buy yourself a pair of washing-up gloves if you can't handle the heat. The hotter the water, the greater likelihood there will be of killing germs.
- Empty bins regularly – they are magnets for bugs, especially during the summer.
- Try not to leave food out (and yes, that even includes dirty plates, even when you're really tired) because the smell can attract mice and flies.
- Defrost meat in the refrigerator, rather than leaving it out on work surfaces.
- Put tea towels and cloths in the wash regularly – they are another breeding ground for germs.
- If something looks or smells bad, don't eat it (unless, of course, like Camembert, the bad smell is part of its culinary charm).

## HONE YOUR TECHNIQUE

If you have spent much of your life avoiding the kitchen, except to eat, then it's time to roll up your sleeves and get to grips with a few basic cooking techniques. Nothing wows a potential mate like the sight of someone expertly chopping garlic and juggling pans without breaking into a sweat. Even if you learn how to prepare only a couple of key recipes, you know you've always got something up your sleeve for a romantic night in or for a rowdy, food-based gathering with your mates. If you are a complete novice when it comes to the kitchen, here are a few terms and techniques to give your culinary confidence a boost.

### Pare

This isn't to be confused with the fruit! It's the

way you peel the skin from a piece of fruit or a vegetable, using a paring knife.

**Beat**

If you want fluffy eggs you're going to have to beat the hell out of them. You need a firm arm, a good wrist movement and a lot of patience for this. You can use a fork for scrambling or a food whisk if you're trying to create magic by transforming sloppy egg whites into fluffy clouds.

**Marinate**

If you leave your fish fillets or chicken portions to soak in a sauce for a while before cooking them, congratulations - you've just marinated. It's a way of getting extra flavour into your food, and can be anything from olive oil and lemon juice to jerk seasoning or barbecue sauce.

**Baste**

Here you marinate the meat first then brush it with the marinade while it's cooking. It helps to add flavour and keep the meat moist.

**Season**

Seasoning is mainly about adding salt and pepper to a recipe for maximum flavour. The key is to add a little at a time and taste as you go along. You can also season with spices and other condiments - the recipes will let you know what you need.

**Purée**

This is mash with muscles and the only way to guarantee you don't end up with lumps in your spuds. You can push the cooked potatoes through a sieve or use a food processor. You can also purée other vegetables, such as carrots or peas, for classy side dishes that are easy to whip up.

**Chop**

This is just another word for 'cut', but some things need to be chopped into big chunks, while other ingredients require a more delicate and precise hand. If real precision is called for, chop becomes 'dice'.

**Poach**

You've probably come across a poached egg before (if not, you really shouldn't be left unsupervised with raw ingredients and sharp knives), but you can also poach fish and chicken. It's a gentle way of cooking food in water, milk or other liquid so that it stays moist and tender.

**Simmer**

Liquid that's bubbling over the side of the pan can be quite aggressive towards delicate food, but simmering treats food with a little more respect. Simmering should stop your boiled eggs from cracking and your sauces from burning on the bottom of the pan.

**Fillet**

The butcher, fishmonger or supermarket will have generally done this way before you get to the stage of handling your ingredients, but if you really want a second date make sure your prospective partner is idling in the kitchen while you skilfully remove the fillets from a mackerel.

**Blanch**

Involves giving your vegetables the merest hint of contact with a pan of boiling water. Cook vegetables like broccoli and carrots for just a few minutes to retain more of their nutrients and taste better too. (Let's leave the over-boiled, grey vegetable medley to nursing homes, shall we?)

## SITTING ON THE SHELF

There are some basic ingredients that crop up time and again in recipes so it makes sense to have a stockpile of these in your cupboard. That way, you will always have the makings of something nutritious. Condiments, sauces, dried herbs and spices last a long time so it's worth making a list before you move in and getting everyone to buy a few things to give your store cupboard a boost. Here's what every self-respecting kitchen should contain:

**Salt and pepper**

Fine and ground respectively for everyday, or sea salt and peppercorns to impress.

### Chopped tomatoes

These are essential for sauces, soups and stews. They are cheap, nutritious and versatile.

### Oil

Vegetable oil is the budget go-to oil of choice, but olive oil doesn't cost much more and it's great for dressings, marinades and sauces as well as for cooking.

### Butter (or spread)

Because toast provides a disproportionate number of the average student's daily calories, you must always have a supply of spread ... and whatever else you like to slather on your bread.

### Onions and garlic

These vegetables are the basics of pretty much every Indian and Italian soup, curry and sauce. They add heaps of flavour and are also good for battling cold and bugs.

### Rice

When there's nothing fresh in the refrigerator you can always rustle up a plate of spicy rice. Choose brown for health, arborio for risottos and jasmine for Thai food.

### Pasta

It's a cliché, but many a student has avoided malnutrition thanks to a sturdy pasta jar. Pick one or two types - spaghetti and penne, for instance - so that you don't end up with loads of almost empty bags of random shapes.

### Cans of beans

You don't need to stick to baked beans. Broaden your culinary horizons by stocking up on other cheap, protein-rich varieties like kidney beans (great for chillies), borlotti and butter beans (for adding bulk to soups) and chickpeas (perfect for stews, curries and salads).

### Canned fish

Another must-have staple. You can live through nuclear fallout if you've got enough cans of tuna and salmon in your store cupboard. Think baked potatoes, pasta, salads and sandwiches.

## GOING GOURMET

As you pick your way through this book, you will first be mystified, then intrigued and eventually (we hope) fluent in cookery speak and able to master a recipe the first time you try it. The recipes have been designed to treat you with the brains you were born with. They assume that the fact you've arrived at university means you have some previous knowledge of books and the modicum of intelligence required to follow a set of simple instructions through to their delicious conclusion.

It's time to buck the trend of generations of kitchen-shy students who survived on cold beans and treat yourself and your housemates to decent dinners. Good luck and enjoy.

## BUDGETING

Boring as it may be, unless you want to spend the last month of each term hiding in your hovel and eating plain rice, budgeting is a necessary part of student life. Each recipe in this book is rated from 1 to 3, with 1s providing end-of-term saviours that can be scraped together for a pittance, and 3s to splash out and impress all your friends.

YELLOW CURRY CHICKEN
WITH PINEAPPLE

TUNA ARRABIATA

MAPLE-GLAZED CHICKEN

# PHD
## IN ONE POT

CHICKEN & SPINACH MASALA

# CHUNKY CHORIZO, PASTA & BEAN SOUP

4 tablespoons extra virgin olive oil
1 large onion, chopped
50 g (2 oz) chorizo sausage, chopped
4 garlic cloves, crushed
2 tablespoons chopped thyme
750 ml (1⅓ pints) Chicken Stock (see page 234)
1.2 litres (2 pints) passata (sieved tomatoes)
2 x 400 g (13 oz) cans borlotti beans, rinsed and drained
200 g (7 oz) small pasta shapes, such as conchigliette
3 tablespoons chopped basil
salt and pepper
grated Parmesan cheese, to serve

Serves **4**
Prep time **10 minutes**
Cooking time **30 minutes**

1 Heat the oil in a saucepan and fry the onion, chorizo, garlic and thyme for 5 minutes. Meanwhile, heat the stock in a separate saucepan.

2 Add the hot stock, passata, beans and salt and pepper to the onion mixture and bring to the boil. Reduce the heat, cover and simmer for 15 minutes.

3 Stir in the pasta and basil and cook for a further 8–10 minutes until the pasta is tender. Adjust the seasoning if necessary, then spoon into warmed bowls and serve topped with grated Parmesan.

AFFORDABILITY
2

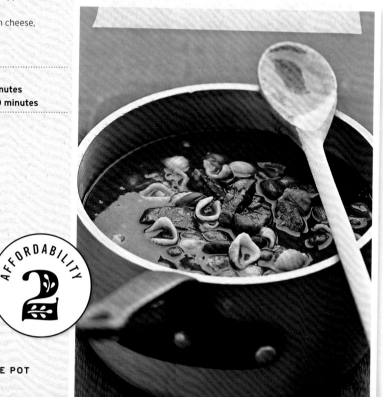

# SMOKED HADDOCK CHOWDER

1 Cut the tops off the bread rolls and pull out the soft centres, leaving a bowl shape and a lid. Place on a baking sheet in a preheated oven, 160°C (325°F), Gas Mark 3, and bake for 25 minutes until they have dried out and become crispy. Brush the inside of the bread rolls with the egg. Put the rolls back in the oven for a further 5 minutes to dry out once again. Remove from the oven and set aside.

2 Heat the butter in a large saucepan, add the spring onions and fry until soft. Add the garlic and potatoes and fry for a further minute. Pour in the milk, cream and stock and bring the soup to the boil, then reduce the heat and simmer for 10 minutes or until the potatoes are almost cooked.

3 Add the sweetcorn and smoked haddock to the pan and simmer for a further 5 minutes until the fish has cooked. Season with salt and pepper.

4 Heat the oil in a frying pan and fry the bacon until crispy. When ready to serve, place the bread bowls in shallow bowls. Pour the soup into the bread bowls, then top with the bacon and a sprinkling of parsley.

4 large round white bread rolls
1 egg, lightly beaten
50 g (2 oz) butter
8 spring onions chopped
1 garlic clove, crushed
2 large, waxy potatoes, peeled and cubed
350 ml (12 fl oz) milk
200 ml (7 fl oz) double cream
200 ml (7 fl oz) Fish Stock (see page 235)
250 g (8 oz) can sweetcorn, drained
500 g (1 lb) smoked haddock, skinned and cut into large chunks
1 tablespoon olive oil
8 streaky bacon rashers, chopped
salt and pepper
2 tablespoons chopped parsley, to garnish

Serves **4**
Prep time **15 minutes**
Cooking time **30 minutes**

3 tablespoons olive oil
1 onion, finely chopped
2 celery sticks, thinly sliced
2 garlic cloves, thinly sliced
2 x 425 g (14 oz) cans butter
  beans, rinsed and drained
4 tablespoons sun-dried tomato
  paste
900 ml (1½ pints) Vegetable Stock
  (see page 235)
1 tablespoon chopped rosemary or
  thyme, plus extra to serve
salt and pepper
Parmesan cheese shavings, to
  serve

Serves **4**
Prep time **5 minutes**
Cooking time **20 minutes**

# BUTTER BEAN
## *&* SUN-DRIED
TOMATO SOUP

1 Heat the oil in a saucepan, add the onion and fry for
3 minutes until softened. Add the celery and garlic and fry
for 2 minutes.

2 Add the butter beans, tomato paste, stock, rosemary or
thyme and a little salt and pepper. Bring to the boil, then
reduce the heat, cover and simmer gently for 15 minutes. Serve
sprinkled with the Parmesan shavings.

# ROAST ROOT VEGETABLE SOUP

**1** Put the carrots and parsnips in a roasting tin, spray lightly with olive oil and season with salt and pepper. Roast in a preheated oven, 200°C (400°F), Gas Mark 6, for 1 hour or until the vegetables are very soft.

**2** Meanwhile, 20 minutes before the vegetables have finished roasting, put the leeks in a large saucepan with the stock and 1 teaspoon of the thyme. Cover the pan and simmer for 20 minutes.

**3** Transfer the roasted root vegetables to a blender or food processor and blend, adding a little of the stock if necessary. Transfer to the stock saucepan and season to taste. Add the remaining thyme, stir and simmer for 5 minutes to reheat.

**4** Ladle into individual bowls and serve garnished with the thyme sprigs.

4 carrots, chopped
2 parsnips, chopped
olive oil, for spraying
1 leek, finely chopped
1.2 litres (2 pints) Vegetable Stock
 (see page 235)
2 teaspoons thyme leaves
salt and pepper
thyme sprigs, to garnish

Serves **6**
Prep time **10 minutes**
Cooking time **1 hour 5 minutes**

AFFORDABILITY
1

# CHEAT'S CURRIED VEGETABLE SOUP

2 tablespoons sunflower oil
1 onion, finely chopped
2 garlic cloves, finely chopped
4 teaspoons mild curry paste
2.5 cm (1 inch) piece of fresh root ginger, peeled and grated
2 small baking potatoes, diced
2 carrots, diced
1 small cauliflower, core discarded, florets cut into small pieces
75 g (3 oz) red lentils
1.5 litres (2½ pints) Vegetable or Chicken Stock (see pages 234 and 235)
400 g (13 oz) can chopped tomatoes
200 g (7 oz) spinach leaves, rinsed and any large leaves torn into pieces
naan bread, to serve (optional)

**Raita**
150 ml (¼ pint) low-fat natural yogurt
4 tablespoons chopped fresh coriander leaves
4 teaspoons mango chutney

Serves **6**
Prep time **25 minutes**
Cooking time **40 minutes**

1 Heat the oil in a large saucepan, add the onion and fry for 5 minutes, stirring until softened. Stir in the garlic, curry paste and ginger and cook for 1 minute.

2 Mix in the potatoes, carrots, cauliflower and lentils. Pour in the stock and tomatoes, season with salt and pepper and bring to the boil. Cover and simmer for 30 minutes or until the lentils are tender.

3 Meanwhile, make the raita. Mix together the yogurt, coriander and mango chutney and spoon into a small bowl.

4 Add the spinach to the soup and cook for 2 minutes until just wilted. Taste and adjust the seasoning if needed. Ladle the soup into shallow bowls and top with spoonfuls of raita. Serve with warmed naan bread, if liked.

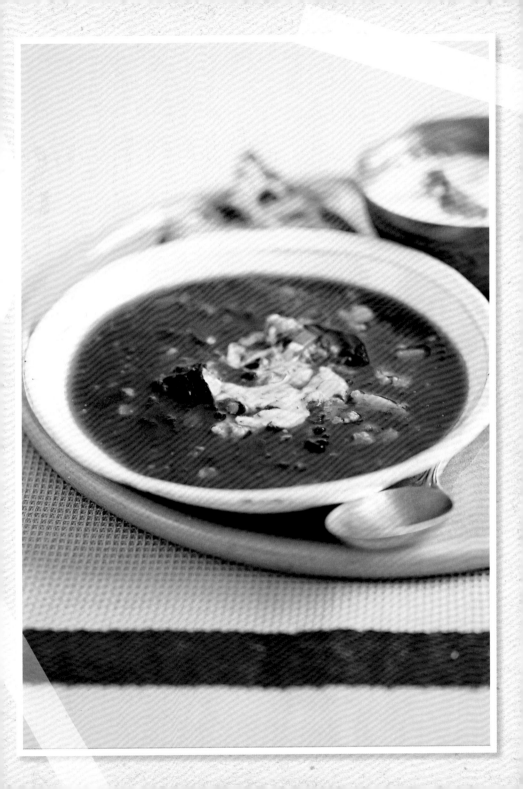

# MAPLE-GLAZED *Chicken*

4 chicken thigh and drumstick
  joints
2 dessert apples, cored, quartered
250 g (8 oz) shallots, peeled,
  halved if large
625 g (1¼ lb) parsnips, quartered
6 bay leaves
2 tablespoons olive oil
2 tablespoons maple syrup
2 tablespoons cider vinegar
salt and pepper
rocket salad, to serve (optional)

Serves **4**
Prep time **15 minutes**
Cooking time **40-45 minutes**

**1** Slash the chicken joints 3-4 times and put them into a large roasting tin with the apples, shallots, parsnips and bay leaves.

**2** Mix the remaining ingredients together and spoon over the chicken and vegetables. Add 4 tablespoons water to the base of the tin. Cook in a preheated oven, 190°C (375°F), Gas Mark 5, for 40-45 minutes, spooning the glaze over the chicken once or twice until deep brown and cooked through.

**3** Spoon on to plates and serve with a rocket salad, if liked.

AFFORDABILITY **2**

# CHICKEN WITH CORNMEAL DUMPLINGS

**1** Heat the oil in a large, shallow flameproof casserole and fry the chicken pieces for about 5 minutes until lightly browned. Stir in the spice blend and cook for a further minute. Drain to a plate.

**2** Add the onion, bacon and peppers and fry, stirring frequently, for 10 minutes or until beginning to colour.

**3** Return the chicken to the casserole and stir in the stock and a little seasoning. Bring to the boil, cover with a lid and bake in a preheated oven, 180°C (350°F), Gas Mark 4, for 45 minutes until the chicken is tender.

**4** Meanwhile, prepare the dumplings. Mix together the flour, cornmeal, chilli flakes, coriander and cheese in a bowl. Beat the butter with the egg and milk and add to the bowl. Mix together to make a thick paste that is fairly sticky but holds its shape.

**5** Stir the tomatoes and cream into the chicken mixture and season to taste. Put spoonfuls of the dumpling mixture over the top. Return to the oven, uncovered, for a further 30 minutes or until the dumplings have slightly risen and formed a firm crust.

3 tablespoons olive oil
8 boneless, skinless chicken thighs, cut into small pieces
4 teaspoons Cajun spice blend
1 large onion, sliced
100 g (3½ oz) smoked streaky bacon, chopped
2 red peppers, deseeded and roughly chopped
2 yellow peppers, deseeded and roughly chopped
200 ml (7 fl oz) Chicken Stock (see page 234)
4 small tomatoes, skinned and quartered
100 ml (3½ fl oz) double cream
salt and pepper

**Dumplings**
125 g (4 oz) self-raising flour
125 g (4 oz) cornmeal
½ teaspoon dried chilli flakes
3 tablespoons chopped fresh coriander
75 g (3 oz) Cheddar cheese, grated
50 g (2 oz) butter, melted
1 egg
100 ml (3½ fl oz) milk

Serves **4**
Prep time **25 minutes**
Cooking time 1½ **hours**

# CHICKEN KORMA

2 tablespoons sunflower oil
8 boneless, skinless chicken
   thighs, about 1 kg (2 lb) in total,
   cubed
2 onions, finely chopped, plus
   extra to garnish
1-2 green chillies (to taste),
   deseeded and finely chopped
2.5 cm (1 inch) fresh root ginger,
   peeled and finely chopped
5 tablespoons korma curry paste
250 ml (8 fl oz) coconut cream or
   milk
300 ml (½ pint) Chicken Stock
   (see page 234)
2 tablespoons ground almonds
small bunch of fresh coriander
200 ml (7 fl oz) natural yogurt
2 tomatoes, diced
salt and pepper
chapattis, to serve

1 Heat the oil in a large frying pan, add the chicken a few
pieces at time until it is all in the pan and fry, stirring, until
golden. Remove from the pan with a slotted spoon and transfer
to a flameproof casserole.

2 Add the onions, green chillies, ginger and curry paste to
the pan and fry, stirring, for 2-3 minutes. Pour in the
coconut cream or milk, stock and ground almonds. Tear half the
coriander into pieces and add to the sauce with a little salt and
pepper. Bring to the boil, stirring, then spoon over the chicken.
Cover with the lid and cook over a low heat for 30-40 minutes
or until the chicken is cooked through.

3 Stir the korma then ladle into bowls, top with spoonfuls of
yogurt, tomatoes and extra raw onion and the remaining
coriander torn into small pieces. Serve with warm chapattis.

Serves **4**
Prep time **20 minutes**
Cooking time **45-55 minutes**

## Cool down your curry

If you get a bit carried away
with your chillies, and you've
made a curry that will blow
your mates' heads off, don't
despair. Remove some of the
sauce (you can freeze this
for next time) and add a can
of chopped tomatoes, some
coconut milk or natural yogurt
to the remaining sauce.

AFFORDABILITY
2

AFFORDABILITY

# CARIBBEAN CHICKEN
# WITH RICE & PEAS

**1** Remove the skin from the chicken thighs, slash each thigh two or three times and rub with the jerk marinade.

**2** Heat 1 tablespoon oil in a large frying pan, add the chicken and fry over a high heat until browned on both sides. Lift out with a slotted spoon and transfer to a plate. Add the remaining oil, the onions and garlic, reduce the heat and fry for 5 minutes or until softened and lightly browned. Pour in the coconut milk and stock, season with salt and pepper and bring to the boil.

**3** Transfer the mixture to a flameproof casserole and add the chicken, the beans and the onion and coconut mixture. Stir to mix, cover, cook over a low heat for 20 minutes until the chicken is cooked through and tender.

**4** Stir in the rice, replace the lid and cook over a high heat for 15 minutes. Add the frozen peas (no need to thaw) and cook for a further 5 minutes. Spoon on to plates and serve garnished with lime wedges and coriander sprigs.

8 chicken thighs, about 1 kg (2 lb) in total
3 tablespoons jerk marinade
2 tablespoons sunflower oil
2 large onions, chopped
2 garlic cloves, finely chopped
400 ml (14 fl oz) can full-fat coconut milk
300 ml (½ pint) Chicken Stock (see page 234)
410 g (13½ oz) can red kidney beans, drained
200 g (7 oz) easy-cook long grain rice
125 g (4 oz) frozen peas
salt and pepper

**To garnish**
lime wedges
fresh coriander sprigs

Serves **4**
Prep time **20 minutes**
Cooking time **55-60 minutes**

# SAUSAGE & SWEET POTATO **HASH**

3 tablespoons olive oil
8 pork sausages
3 large red onions, thinly sliced
1 teaspoon caster sugar
500 g (1 lb) sweet potatoes, scrubbed and cut into small chunks
8 sage leaves
2 tablespoons balsamic vinegar
salt and pepper

Serves **4**
Prep time **15 minutes**
Cooking time **45 minutes**

**1** Heat the oil in a large frying pan or flameproof casserole and fry the sausages, turning frequently, for about 10 minutes or until browned. Drain to a plate.

**2** Add the onions and sugar to the pan and cook gently, stirring frequently, until lightly browned. Return the sausages to the pan and add the sweet potatoes, sage leaves and a little seasoning.

**3** Cover the pan with a lid or kitchen foil and cook over a very gentle heat for about 25 minutes until the potatoes are tender.

**4** Drizzle with the vinegar, check the seasoning and serve.

# BEST
## BRAIN FOOD

You got a place at university so you must have some grey matter floating around between your ears and, whether you're studying medicine or the benefits of floatation techniques, at least you've made it. However, with thousands of brain cells irreversibly zapped every time you have a big night at the student union, it makes sense to try to preserve those that remain with a few food wins. Here are some of the ingredients that will give you the edge in the lecture theatre.

## OILY FISH

Unfortunately, fish fingers won't cut the mustard: we're talking about salmon, mackerel and tuna if you really want to give your brain a boost. It's the omega 3 acids that you're after, but don't worry if you've got a fish phobia – it's the easiest food in the world to cook. Try Tuna & Pasta Bake (see page 134) for a tasty meal to get you hooked or add some salmon flakes or tuna to sandwiches, pasta sauces or jacket potatoes.

## NUTS & SEEDS

This is where you can get a quick, tasty burst of vitamin E, which helps to protect your cells. Buy a big mixed bag and transfer a handful at a time to a freezer bag or small plastic tub for a daily snack when you're out and about.

## WHOLEGRAINS

Unfortunately, you really should try to avoid cheap white bread and shuffle up next to the healthy shoppers in the wholemeal section instead. When it comes to bread, the more grains the better, and switching to brown rice and wholemeal pasta, or to porridge for breakfast, will make sure you get plenty of fibre, vitamins and slow-burning carbs into your diet.

## EGGS

As they are a student staple, you probably have a fair number of eggs in your diet already, but isn't it nice to know that they're good for your brain too? For extra points, try getting your eggs by poaching, boiling or scrambling them rather than in a fry-up at your local greasy spoon.

## CHOCOLATE

This isn't an excuse to swap meals for sweets, but when it comes to chocolate a little of what you fancy really does do you good. You need to be a bit more discerning in your buying habits though, because it's plain dark chocolate that has the most antioxidants and flavonoids (technical terms for healthy things). But don't forget that all chocolate contains heaps of sugar so you need to rein in your sweet tooth and treat it, well, like a treat.

# EASY
## SAUSAGE
### *&* BEANS

1 tablespoon sunflower oil
1 onion, chopped
½ teaspoon smoked paprika
2 x 410 g (13½ oz) cans baked
  beans
2 teaspoons wholegrain mustard
2 tablespoons Worcestershire
  sauce
6 tablespoons Vegetable Stock
  (see page 235)
2 tomatoes, roughly chopped
½ red pepper, cored, deseeded
  and diced
350 g (11½ oz) chilled frankfurters,
  thickly sliced
salt and pepper
buttered toast, to serve

1 Heat the oil in a frying pan, add the onion and fry, stirring, for 5 minutes or until softened and just beginning to turn golden.

2 Stir in the paprika and cook for 1 minute, then mix in the beans, mustard, Worcestershire sauce and stock. Bring to the boil, then stir in the tomatoes, red pepper and a little salt and pepper.

3 Put the frankfurters in a flameproof casserole and tip the baked bean mixture over the top. Cover with the lid and cook over a low heat for 40-45 minutes, stirring occasionally.

4 Stir well, spoon into shallow bowls and serve with buttered toast fingers.

Serves **4**
Prep time **15 minutes**
Cooking time **50-55 minutes**

# Creamy Pork & CIDER HOTPOT

1 Cut the pork into small pieces, discarding any excess fat. Season the flour with a little salt and use to coat the meat.

2 Melt the butter with the oil in a shallow, flameproof casserole and gently fry the pork, in batches, until lightly browned, draining each batch to a plate.

3 Add the onion and leek to the casserole and fry gently for 5 minutes. Return the meat to the pan, along with the cider, sage and mustard. Bring just to the boil, cover with a lid, reduce the heat and cook on the lowest setting for 30 minutes.

4 Stir the crème fraîche into the sauce and scatter the pear slices on top. Arrange the sweet potato slices in overlapping layers on top, putting the end pieces underneath and keeping the best slices for the top layer. Brush with the chilli oil and sprinkle with salt.

5 Cook in a preheated oven, 160ºC (325ºF), Gas Mark 3, for 45 minutes or until the potatoes are tender and lightly browned. Scatter with the chopped parsley before serving.

625 g (1¼ lb) lean, boneless leg of pork
2 teaspoons plain flour
25 g (1 oz) butter
1 tablespoon oil
1 small onion, chopped
1 large leek, chopped
450 ml (¾ pint) cider
1 tablespoon chopped sage
2 tablespoons grainy mustard
100 ml (3½ fl oz) crème fraîche
2 pears, peeled, cored and thickly sliced
450 g (14½ oz) sweet potatoes, scrubbed and thinly sliced
2 tablespoons chilli-infused oil
salt
chopped parsley, to garnish

Serves **4**
Prep time **25 minutes**
Cooking time **1½ hours**

AFFORDABILITY
2

# Cassoulet

IN A GOOD CASSOULET THE BEANS TURN SOFT AND CREAMY AND THICKEN THE MEATY JUICES.

625 g (1¼ lb) dried haricot beans, soaked overnight in water
4 tablespoons olive oil or goose fat
750 g (1½ lb) piece belly pork, skinned and cut into chunks
4 duck legs, halved
8 garlicky sausages
2 onions, chopped
2 bay leaves
1.2 litres (2 pints) Chicken Stock (see page 234)
4 garlic cloves, crushed
good pinch of ground cloves
3 tablespoons tomato paste
75 g (3 oz) fresh breadcrumbs
salt and pepper

Serves **6**
Prep time **30 minutes, plus soaking**
Cooking time **about 3½ hours**

1 Drain the beans and put them in a large saucepan. Cover them with cold water, bring to the boil and cook rapidly for 10 minutes. Reduce the heat and simmer gently for 30 minutes until slightly softened. Drain.

2 Heat the oil or fat in a large, heavy-based frying pan, add the pork pieces and fry, in batches, until lightly browned. Drain and fry the duck pieces and sausages until browned.

3 Tip half the beans into a large earthenware pot or casserole dish and scatter over half the meat, half the chopped onions and the bay leaves. Add the remaining beans, meat and onions.

4 Blend the stock with the garlic, cloves and tomato paste and pour the mixture over the beans. Season to taste. Top up with a little water so that the beans are nearly submerged, cover and cook in a preheated oven, 160°C (325°F), Gas Mark 3, for 2 hours until the beans are completely tender.

5 Scatter the breadcrumbs over the surface and return to the oven, uncovered, for a further 30-40 minutes until golden.

# *Spaghetti* CARBONARA

1 Heat the oil in a saucepan, add the bacon and cook gently for 3 minutes. Add the garlic and cook for a further minute.

2 Bring a large saucepan of salted water to the boil and cook the spaghetti for 3–4 minutes if fresh or 8 minutes if dried or according to the pack instructions. Drain and return the pasta to the pan.

3 Beat the cream and egg yolks together in a bowl, add to the bacon and mix well over a low heat.

4 Add the sauce and Parmesan to the pasta, season with salt and pepper and toss well. Serve immediately.

1 tablespoon olive oil
175 g (6 oz) smoked bacon, rinded and cut into strips
1 garlic clove, crushed
300 g (10 oz) spaghetti
4 tablespoons double cream
3 egg yolks
75 g (3 oz) Parmesan cheese, grated
salt and pepper

Serves **4**
Prep time **10 minutes**
Cooking time **15 minutes**

AFFORDABILITY
2

### Bin the brands

You might be used to your mum spoiling you with expensive beans and cereal but you've got to fend for yourself now – beans or beer? If you switch to supermarket own-brand ingredients you could save a fortune on your shopping bills. Often, own-brand ingredients taste just as good as branded ones, but it will take some trial and error to find out which brands you're happy to bin and which you simply can't live without.

# Chilli
# CON CARNE

2 tablespoon olive oil
1 red onion, finely chopped
3 garlic cloves, finely chopped
250 g (8 oz) lean minced beef
½ teaspoon ground cumin
1 small red pepper, deseeded and diced
400 g (13 oz) can chopped tomatoes
1 tablespoon tomato purée
2 teaspoons mild chilli powder
200 ml (7 fl oz) Beef Stock (see page 234)
400 g (13 oz) can red kidney beans, rinsed and drained
salt and pepper
brown rice, to serve

Serves **2**
Prep time **15 minutes**
Cooking time **45 minutes**

1 Heat the oil in a saucepan, add the onion and garlic and cook for 5 minutes or until beginning to soften. Add the mince and cumin and cook for a further 5-6 minutes or until browned all over.

2 Stir in the red pepper, tomatoes, tomato purée, chilli powder and stock and bring to the boil. Reduce the heat and simmer gently for 30 minutes.

3 Add the beans and cook for a further 5 minutes. Season to taste and serve with brown rice, cooked according to the pack instructions.

# BOLOGNESE SAUCE

COMBINING ITALIAN-STYLE SPICY SAUSAGES WITH THE MORE FAMILIAR MINCED BEEF GIVES THIS SAUCE A RICH MEATY FLAVOUR REMINISCENT OF THE TRADITIONAL SAUCE SERVED IN BOLOGNA.

1 Melt the butter with the oil in a large, heavy-based saucepan and gently fry the onion and celery for 5 minutes. Add the garlic, beef and sausages and cook until they are lightly coloured, breaking up the beef and the sausages with a wooden spoon.

2 Add the wine and let it bubble for 1–2 minutes until slightly evaporated. Add the tomatoes, sugar, bay leaves, oregano, tomato paste and a little salt and pepper and bring just to the boil. Reduce the heat to its lowest setting, cover the pan with a lid and cook for about 1 hour, stirring occasionally, until thick and pulpy.

25 g (1 oz) butter
2 tablespoons olive oil
1 onion, finely chopped
2 celery sticks, finely chopped
2 garlic cloves, crushed
500 g (1 lb) lean minced beef
200 g (7 oz) spicy Italian
  sausages, skinned
300 ml (½ pint) red or white wine
400 g (13 oz) can chopped
  tomatoes
1 teaspoon caster sugar
2 bay leaves
1 teaspoon dried oregano
2 tablespoons sun-dried tomato
  paste
salt and pepper

Serves **4-5**
Prep time **15 minutes**
Cooking time **1¼ hours**

AFFORDABILITY
2

# STEAK & ALE CASSEROLE

2 tablespoons plain flour
1 kg (2 lb) braising steak, cut into chunks
25 g (1 oz) butter
1 tablespoon oil
2 onions, chopped
2 celery sticks, sliced
several thyme sprigs
2 bay leaves
400 ml (14 fl oz) strong ale
300 ml (½ pint) Beef Stock (see page 234)
2 tablespoons black treacle
500 g (1 lb) parsnips, peeled and cut into wedges
salt and pepper

Serves **5-6**
Prep time **20 minutes**
Cooking time **1¾ hours**

1 Season the flour with salt and pepper and coat the beef in the flour. Melt the butter with the oil in a large, flameproof casserole and fry the beef, in batches, until deep brown. Drain with a slotted spoon while you cook the remainder.

2 Add the onions and celery and fry gently for 5 minutes. Return the beef to the pan and add the herbs, ale, stock and treacle. Bring just to the boil, reduce the heat and cover with a lid. Bake in a preheated oven, 160ºC (325ºF), Gas Mark 3, for 1 hour.

3 Add the parsnips to the dish and return to the oven for a further 30 minutes or until the beef and parsnips are tender. Check the seasoning and serve.

# STIFADO

**1** Mix together the pepper, allspice and rosemary and rub the mixture over the rabbit.

**2** Heat the oil in a large, flameproof casserole and fry the meat, in batches, on all sides until thoroughly browned. Drain the meat to a plate.

**3** Add the onions to the pan with the sugar and fry, stirring frequently, for about 15 minutes until caramelized. Stir in the garlic and cook for a further minute.

**4** Add the vinegar and wine to the pan. Bring to the boil and continue to boil until the mixture has reduced by about one-third. Stir in the tomato purée and a little salt and return the meat to the pan.

**5** Cover with a lid and place in a preheated oven, 150°C (300°F), Gas Mark 2, for about 2 hours until the meat is very tender and the juices thick and glossy. Check the seasoning and sprinkle with the parsley before serving.

½ teaspoon ground black pepper
½ teaspoon ground allspice
2 teaspoons finely chopped rosemary
1 rabbit, about 750-875 g (1½-1¾ lb), jointed
3 tablespoons olive oil
3 large onions, sliced
2 teaspoons caster sugar
3 garlic cloves, crushed
75 ml (3 fl oz) red wine vinegar
300 ml (½ pint) red wine
50 g (2 oz) tomato purée
salt
flat leaf parsley, to garnish

Serves **3-4**
Prep time **20 minutes**
Cooking time **2½ hours**

AFFORDABILITY
3

# TUNA ARRABIATA

1 tablespoon olive oil
1 onion, chopped
2 garlic cloves, finely chopped
1 red pepper, cored, deseeded and
   diced
1 teaspoon smoked paprika
¼–½ teaspoon crushed dried red
   chillies
400 g (13 oz) can chopped
   tomatoes
150 ml (⅓ pint) Vegetable or Fish
   Stock (see page 235)
200 g (7 oz) can tuna in water,
   drained
375 g (12 oz) spaghetti
salt and pepper

**To serve**
grated Parmesan cheese
basil leaves

Serves **4**
Prep time **20 minutes**
Cooking time **20-25 minutes**

1 Heat the oil in a frying pan, add the onion and fry, stirring, for 5 minutes or until just beginning to turn golden around the edges.

2 Stir in the garlic, red pepper, paprika and dried chillies and cook for 2 minutes. Add the tomatoes, stock and a little salt and pepper. Bring to the boil, then transfer to a flameproof casserole. Break the tuna into large pieces and stir into the tomato mixture. Cover with the lid and cook over a low heat for 10-15 minutes.

3 When you are almost ready to serve, bring a large saucepan of salted water to the boil, add the spaghetti and cook for about 8 minutes until tender or according to the pack instructions. Drain and stir into the tomato sauce to coat the pasta. Spoon into shallow bowls and sprinkle with grated Parmesan and basil leaves to taste.

# SPINACH & MUSHROOM *Lasagne*

AFFORDABILITY **1**

1 Make the sauce. Put the milk and bay leaves in a saucepan and heat to boiling point. Remove from the heat and leave to infuse for 20 minutes. Discard the bay leaves.

2 Melt the butter in a separate saucepan, add the flour and cook over a medium heat, stirring constantly, for 1 minute. Gradually stir in the milk and continue to cook, stirring, until the mixture boils. Reduce the heat and simmer for 2 minutes. Remove from the heat, add most of the Cheddar and stir until melted.

3 Meanwhile, heat the oil in a frying pan, add the garlic, thyme, mushrooms and salt and pepper and cook over a medium heat, stirring frequently, for 5 minutes until tender. Squeeze out the excess water from the spinach and roughly chop. Stir into the mushroom mixture, then remove from the heat.

4 Lightly oil a 2.5 litre (4 pint) lasagne dish with spray oil. Spread a quarter of the cheese sauce over the base and add one-third of the mushroom and spinach mixture and a lasagne sheet. Repeat these layers twice more. Add a final layer of sauce to cover the lasagne and scatter over the remaining cheese. Bake in a preheated oven, 190°C (375°F), Gas Mark 5, for 35-40 minutes until browned.

4 tablespoons olive oil
2 garlic cloves, crushed
2 teaspoons chopped thyme
500 g (1 lb) button mushrooms, trimmed and sliced
500 g (1 lb) frozen leaf spinach (thawed)
spray oil, for oiling
200 g (7 oz) fresh lasagne sheets
salt and black pepper

**Cheese sauce**
1.2 litres (2 pints) milk
2 fresh bay leaves
50 g (2 oz) unsalted butter, plus extra for greasing
50 g (2 oz) plain flour
250 g (8 oz) Cheddar cheese, grated

Serves **6-8**
Prep time **35 minutes, plus infusing**
Cooking time **45-50 minutes**

# SPINACH & GREEN BEAN RISOTTO

1 litre (1¾ pints) vegetable stock
125 g (4 oz) butter
1 tablespoon olive oil
1 garlic clove, crushed and
  chopped
1 onion, finely diced
300 g (10 oz) arborio or carnaroli
  rice
125 g (4 oz) green beans, trimmed
  and cut into short lengths
125 g (4 oz) shelled peas
125 g (4 oz) shelled broad beans
125 g (4 oz) asparagus, trimmed
  and cut into short lengths
125 g (4 oz) baby spinach, chopped
75 ml (3 fl oz) dry vermouth or
  white wine
2 tablespoons chopped parsley
125 g (4 oz) Parmesan cheese,
  freshly grated
salt and pepper

Serves **4**
Prep time **10 minutes**
Cooking time **20 minutes**

1 Place the stock in a saucepan on a low heat until it simmers gently.

2 Melt half of the butter with the oil in a heavy-based saucepan, add the garlic and onion and sauté gently for 5 minutes.

3 Add the rice and stir well to coat each grain with the butter and oil. Add enough stock to just cover the rice and stir well. Simmer gently, stirring frequently.

4 When most of the liquid is absorbed, add more stock and stir well. Continue adding the stock in stages and stirring until it is absorbed. Add the vegetables and vermouth or wine with the final amount of stock, mix well and cook for 2 minutes.

5 Remove the pan from the heat, season and add the remaining butter, parsley and Parmesan. Mix well and serve at once.

AFFORDABILITY
2

# BASIL & TOMATO STEW

AFFORDABILITY
1

1 kg (2 lb) ripe tomatoes, skinned
6 tablespoons olive oil
2 onions, chopped
4 celery sticks, sliced
4 plump garlic cloves, thinly sliced
175 g (6 oz) mushrooms, sliced
3 tablespoons sun-dried tomato paste
600 ml (1 pint) Vegetable Stock (see page 235)
1 tablespoon muscovado sugar
3 tablespoons capers
large handful of basil leaves, about 15 g (½ oz) large handful of chervil or flat leaf parsley, about 15 g (½ oz)
salt and pepper
warm bread, to serve

**1** Quarter and deseed the tomatoes, scooping out the pulp into a sieve over a bowl to catch the juices.

**2** Heat 4 tablespoons oil in a large saucepan and fry the onions and celery for 5 minutes. Add the garlic and mushrooms and fry for a further 3 minutes.

**3** Add the tomatoes and their juices, the sun-dried tomato paste, stock, sugar and capers and bring to the boil. Reduce the heat and simmer gently, uncovered, for 5 minutes.

**4** Tear the herbs into pieces, add to the pan with a little salt and pepper and cook for 1 minute. Ladle into bowls, drizzle with the remaining oil and serve with warm bread.

Serves **4**
Prep time **10 minutes**
Cooking time **15 minutes**

## Peeling garlic

A quick way to prepare garlic is to squash the bulb swiftly with the flat of your hand or under the flat blade of a large knife. The skin will come away easily, and you can chop, crush or add the whole clove to your recipe, according to the recipe.

# BUTTERED
## CAULIFLOWER
# CRUMBLE

1 Cut the cauliflower into large florets and blanch in boiling water for 2 minutes. Drain the florets thoroughly.

2 Melt half the butter in a large frying pan, add the breadcrumbs and fry for 2 minutes until golden. Drain and set aside.

3 Melt the remaining butter in the pan with the oil, add the cauliflower florets and fry gently for about 5 minutes until golden. Add the capers, gherkins, dill or tarragon and crème fraîche, season to taste with salt and pepper and stir the mixture over a moderate heat for 1 minute.

4 Turn into a shallow flameproof dish and sprinkle with the fried breadcrumbs and Parmesan. Cook under a preheated moderate grill for about 2 minutes until the crumbs are dark golden brown.

1 large cauliflower
25 g (1 oz) butter
50 g (2 oz) fresh breadcrumbs
2 tablespoons olive oil
3 tablespoons capers
3 cocktail gherkins, finely chopped
3 tablespoons chopped dill or tarragon
100 ml (3½ fl oz) crème fraîche
4 tablespoons grated Parmesan cheese
salt and pepper

Serves **4**
Prep time **8 minutes**
Cooking time **12 minutes**

# OUTDOOR
# GRUB

GREEK-STYLE
FETA SALAD

VEGETABLE KEBABS WITH PILAF

COLESLAW

BAKED TORTILLAS WITH HUMMUS

# LEMON & HERB BARBECUED CHICKEN WINGS

AFFORDABILITY

2

2 garlic cloves, crushed
grated rind and juice of
  1 lemon
4 thyme sprigs
6 tablespoons extra virgin olive
  oil
1 tablespoon clear honey
1 teaspoon dried oregano
1 teaspoon ground cumin
12 chicken wings
salt and pepper

Serves 4
Prep time 5 minutes
Cooking time 15-20 minutes

1 Put the garlic, lemon rind and juice in a bowl, add the thyme, oil, honey, oregano and cumin and season to taste with salt and pepper. Add the chicken wings and stir until well coated.

2 Barbecue or grill the chicken wings for 15-20 minutes, turning and basting until charred and cooked through.

## Barbecue basics

Barbecuing is a skill that needs to be mastered. The main issue is impatience – if you're cooking on coals, give them time to get really hot because they're not ready for food until the flames are out and they're glowing red. Remember, too, that a blackened burger doesn't necessarily mean a cooked burger – always check the food is cooked through before you potentially poison your mates.

# GREEN **CHICKEN** *KEBABS*

FRAGRANT AND BURSTING WITH FLAVOUR, THESE SUCCULENT CHICKEN SKEWERS ARE LOW IN FAT AND MAKE AN EXCELLENT DISH WHEN SERVED WITH A CRISP CUCUMBER AND RED ONION SALAD.

1 Put the yogurt, garlic, ginger, cumin, ground coriander, chilli, chopped herbs and lime juice in a blender and whizz until fairly smooth. Season lightly.

2 Cut the chicken into bite-sized pieces and place in a large mixing bowl. Pour over the spice mixture and toss to coat evenly. Cover with clingfilm and marinate in the refrigerator for 4–6 hours or overnight if time permits.

3 When ready to cook thread the chicken pieces on to eight pre-soaked bamboo skewers. Barbecue for 8–10 minutes, turning frequently, until cooked through and lightly browned. Serve immediately with halves of lime to squeeze over.

100 ml (3½ fl oz) low-fat
  natural yogurt
2 garlic cloves, crushed
2 teaspoons finely grated
  fresh root ginger
2 teaspoons ground cumin
1 teaspoon ground
  coriander
1 green chilli, finely chopped
large handful of chopped
  fresh coriander leaves
small handful of chopped
  mint leaves
juice of 2 limes
sea salt
4 boneless, skinless chicken
  breasts
halves of lime, to serve

Serves 4
Prep time **10 minutes, plus marinating**
Cooking time **15 minutes**

AFFORDABILITY 2

# MINTED **LAMB** KEBABS

IF YOU'RE COOKING THESE ON A BARBECUE MAKE SURE THEY CHILL FOR PLENTY OF TIME TO ENSURE THEY STAY FIRM ON THE GRILL AND DON'T FALL APART.

1 tablespoon chickpea flour
  (besan or gram flour)
625 g (1¼ lb) finely minced lamb
5 tablespoons finely chopped
  mint leaves
3 tablespoons finely chopped
  fresh coriander leaves
2 green chillies, deseeded and
  finely chopped
2 teaspoons ground cumin
1 teaspoon ground coriander
½ small egg, lightly beaten
sunflower oil, to brush
salt and pepper

1 Put the flour, minced lamb, chopped mint and coriander leaves, chillies and the ground spices in a mixing bowl. Season, add the egg and, using your hands, mix until well combined. Cover and chill for 2-3 hours or overnight.

2 Line a large baking sheet with nonstick baking paper. Shape the mixture into 12 balls, flatten slightly and place on the baking sheet. Brush lightly with the oil and bake in a preheated oven, 190ºC (375º F), Gas Mark 5, for 12-15 minutes until cooked through. Remove, thread on to skewers and serve immediately. Alternatively, you can cook the lamb balls over a barbecue, turning occassionally until they are cooked through.

Serves 4
Prep time **15 minutes, plus marinating**
Cooking time **12-15 minutes**

AFFORDABILITY
2

### Wooden skewers

If you're barbecuing or grilling with wooden skewers, soak them in water for about half an hour before it's time to cook. While you expect the odd banger to succumb to the flames on a barbecue, there's no joy to be had in watching the skewers catch light.

# *Shish* KEBABS

1 Mix all the ingredients, except the oil, in a large bowl until smooth. Divide the mixture into six equal-sized, sausage-shaped patties.

2 Make the marinade. Mix together the yogurt, curry powder and garlic in a flat-based dish. Thread the patties on to oiled metal skewers, immerse in the marinade and leave for 2–4 hours.

3 Remove the skewers from the marinade. Brush the patties with oil and cook, turning occasionally, on a medium-hot barbecue for 10–15 minutes.

4 Serve hot with the onion, pepper and parsley, dusted over with paprika, and with lime wedges to squeeze over.

375 g (12 oz) minced lamb
1 onion, finely chopped
2 teaspoons lemon juice
1 egg, beaten
2 tablespoons plain flour
2 tablespoons chopped fresh coriander
½ teaspoon salt
oil, for brushing

**Marinade**
4 tablespoons natural yogurt
1 tablespoon medium or hot curry powder
1 garlic clove, crushed

**To serve**
red onion, finely sliced
red pepper, finely sliced
1 tablespoon chopped parsley
1 teaspoon paprika
lemon wedges

Serves **6**
Prep time **15 minutes, plus marinating**
Cooking time **10–15 minutes**

AFFORDABILITY

# SPICY MAPLE RIBS

THESE ARE GREAT FOR SUMMER PARTIES AND CAN BE PACKED UP AND TAKEN ON A PICNIC. REMEMBER TO BASTE SEVERAL TIMES DURING COOKING TO MAKE THE MOST OF THEIR DELICIOUSLY DARK, STICKY GLAZE.

1.25 kg (2½ lb) meaty pork spare ribs
100 ml (3½ fl oz) maple syrup
2 garlic cloves, crushed
3 tablespoons white wine vinegar
3 tablespoons tomato paste
finely grated rind and juice of 1 lemon
1 red chilli, deseeded and finely chopped
½ teaspoon smoked paprika
salt
lemon or lime halves, to serve

Serves **4**
Prep time **10 minutes, plus marinating**
Cooking time **1½-1¾ hours**

1 Arrange the meat in a single layer in a shallow, non-metallic dish. Mix together the maple syrup, garlic, vinegar, tomato paste, lemon rind and juice, chilli and paprika. Pour the mixture over the ribs, turning them until they are completely coated, cover and marinate in the refrigerator for 4-24 hours.

2 Transfer the ribs to a shallow roasting tin and pour over the excess marinade from the dish. Season lightly with salt and bake in a preheated oven, 180°C (350°F), Gas Mark 4, for 1½-1¾ hours, basting occasionally with the juices, until the meat is tender and the juices are thick and sticky.

3 Transfer to serving plates and serve immediately with lemon or lime halves for squeezing over.

# MUSTARD-GRILLED
## *Sardines*

*THESE DELICIOUSLY SPICY SARDINES ARE GREAT SERVED SIMPLY WITH A FRESH, CRUNCHY SALAD AND LEMON WEDGES FOR SQUEEZING OVER.*

12 sardines
1 tablespoon wholegrain
  mustard
juice of 2 lemons
1 teaspoon chilli powder
1 teaspoon garam masala
salt and pepper
lemon wedges, to serve

Serves 4
Prep time **10 minutes**
Cooking time **6-8 minutes**

**1** Put the sardines on a large work surface and use a sharp knife to make two or three diagonal slashes on both sides of each fish.

**2** In a small bowl mix together the mustard, lemon juice, chilli powder and garam masala. Season to taste and spread this mixture over the fish.

**3** Cook on a medium-hot barbecue for 3-4 minutes on each side or until cooked through. Serve hot with wedges of lemon.

# SALMON WITH FENNEL
## *& Tomatoes*

*FISH IS A FANTASTIC AND REFRESHING SUMMER SUPPER. THESE CAN BE EASILY BARBECUED BY WRAPPING THE FILLETS IN FOIL AFTER COATING.*

**1** Season the salmon fillets generously with salt and pepper and pour over the lemon juice. Set aside.

**2** In a small bowl mix together the oil, vinegar, honey, garlic. Season to taste with salt and pepper. Put the onions, fennel and tomatoes in a large bowl and pour over the oil mixture. Toss to coat thoroughly, then spread out on a baking sheet.

**3** Roast in a preheated oven, 220°C (425°F), Gas Mark 7, for 10 minutes. Add the salmon fillets to the baking sheet and roast for a further 12-15 minutes. Serve the salmon with the roasted vegetables and rice or couscous.

4 salmon fillets, 175-250 g (6-8 oz) each
4 tablespoons lemon juice
4 tablespoons olive oil
1 tablespoon balsamic vinegar
1 tablespoon clear honey
4 garlic cloves, finely chopped
2 red onions, quartered
2 fennel bulbs, quartered
16-20 vine cherry tomatoes
salt and pepper
rice or couscous, to serve

Serves **4**
Prep time **10 minutes**
Cooking time **22-25 minutes**

AFFORDABILITY **3**

# FEEL THE
# BURN

## BEFORE YOU START

Rub a bit of oil over the grill rack before you start to cook. This helps to prevent the food from sticking to the rack.

## SAFETY FIRST

Make sure the barbecue is completely cold before you leave it – a stray spark could mean a frantic call to the fire service later on.

## THE ART OF BARBECUE

It's unlikely that you will be able to afford a swish barbecue on a budget, which means you're going to have to take your chances with charcoal in a tin tub on wobbly legs. If the food's cooked well, it doesn't matter if you procured your cooking vessel on a late-night drunken skip raid, but there are certain rules that need to be followed if you don't want to poison your mates, don't want to lose your facial hair and don't want your burgers to taste (and look) as if they've been excavated from an archaeological dig.

Like any other cooking method, barbecuing is an art, and there's a lot of multi-tasking involved. You have to appear as though you're casually flipping bangers over hot coals, but at the same time you need to swap jokes with your mates and take regular gulps from a can of lager. Get your timings wrong and you could either run out of beer or overcook a sausage. Here are a few tips that should see you wallowing in a sea of praise.

## TAKE YOUR TIME

Exercise a little patience, the secret weapon of the successful barbecue chef. It's always tempting to start cooking the meat before the coals are hot enough, but you should aim to light the coals at least 30 minutes before you cook, which is how long it takes for the flames to die down and the charcoal to be burning hot.

## BIG PARTY?

If you have a small barbecue and a large number of guests, crank up the oven and transfer cooked food to keep it warm while you finish off on the barbie.

## COOK YOUR MEAT THOROUGHLY

If you're worried about cooking times (or just cooking the meat properly), cut larger pieces of meat or burgers in half lengthways.

## SIMPLICITY RULES

Keep it simple. Don't be too ambitious with the food. It's far better to stick to a couple of meat choices, something for veggies and a few simple side dishes. This isn't a gourmet dinner party; it's cooking over fire.

# CHEESE & SPINACH
## *Tart*

50 g (2 oz) butter
1 small onion, finely chopped
1 garlic clove, crushed
2 teaspoons chopped thyme
250 g (8 oz) frozen leaf spinach
  (thawed)
175 ml (6 fl oz) single cream
2 eggs, beaten
25 g (1 oz) Parmesan cheese,
  grated
20 cm (8 inch) frozen pastry
  tart case (cook from frozen)
salt and black pepper
green salad, to serve

Serves **4**
Prep time **10 minutes**
Cooking time **25 minutes**

**1** Melt the butter in a large frying pan, add the onion, garlic, thyme and salt and pepper to taste and cook for 5 minutes. Squeeze out all the excess water from the spinach, add to the pan and cook, stirring, for 2-3 minutes until heated through.

**2** In a bowl beat together the cream, eggs, cheese and a pinch of salt and pepper. Spoon the spinach mixture into the tart case, carefully pour over the cream mixture and bake on a preheated baking sheet in a preheated oven, 200ºC (400ºF), Gas Mark 6, for 20 minutes until set. Serve with a green salad.

# MUSTARD *&* THYME
## SWEET POTATOES

1 Wrap each potato in a double layer of kitchen foil and either place them on the flat plate of a gas barbecue or, using barbecue tongs, set them in among the heated coals of a charcoal barbecue, allowing some of the coals to cover the potatoes. Bake for 40 minutes.

2 Meanwhile, make the butter. Put the butter, mustard, thyme and some pepper in a bowl and mash with a fork until evenly mixed. Set aside.

3 Remove the potatoes from the barbecue (again using tongs) and carefully remove the foil using oven gloves. Cut the potatoes in half and serve topped with the butter.

6 sweet potatoes, about 250 g (8 oz) each, scrubbed

**Mustard and thyme butter**
125 g (4 oz) butter, softened
1 tablespoon wholegrain mustard
1 teaspoon chopped thyme pepper

Serves **6**
Prep time **5 minutes**
Cooking time **40 minutes**

AFFORDABILITY
1

# Barbecued CORN
## WITH CHILLI & LIME

CHARGRILLING CORN GIVES IT A SMOKY FLAVOUR, WHICH IS SET OFF BY THE SPICY CHILLI AND SHARP, TANGY LIME JUICE.

4 ears of corn (or corn-on-the-cob)
1 tablespoon coarse chilli powder
1 tablespoon sea salt
2 limes, halved

Serves 4
Prep time **5 minutes**
Cooking time **8-10 minutes**

1 Neatly remove the husks from the corn and reserve to serve the final dish on.

2 Mix together the chilli powder and sea salt and put on a small plate or saucer.

3 Cook the corn over a medium heat over a barbecue or under a medium-hot grill for 4-5 minutes, turning them around so that they cook all over, until the corn is lightly charred in places. Remove from the heat, dip a lime half in the chilli mixture and squeeze and spread it over the corn to coat evenly. Repeat with the remaining corn and lime and chilli mixture. Set the corn on the reserved husks and eat immediately.

# GUACAMOLE
# WITH TOTOPOS

THIS DELICIOUS DIP IS PREPARED ALL OVER ITS NATIVE MEXICO AND CAN BE SERVED AS A SIDE DISH TO GRILLED MEATS, SALADS AND RICE OR SIMPLY SPOONED OVER ANY KIND OF TACO.

2 large ripe avocados
1 tablespoon finely chopped
  onion
2 serrano or jalapeño chillies,
  finely chopped
2 tablespoons finely chopped
  fresh coriander, plus extra
  leaves to garnish
squeeze of lime juice
salt

**Totopos**
soft corn tortillas
vegetable oil, for brushing

Serves **4**
Prep time **15 minutes**
Cooking time **8-10 minutes**

1 Make the totopos. Brush each side of the tortillas with a little oil and cut into triangles. Arrange on a baking sheet and bake in a preheated oven, 180ºC (350ºF), Gas Mark 4, for 8-10 minutes until crisp. Sprinkle with a little salt and leave to cool on a wire rack.

2 Halve the avocados and remove the stones. Cut the flesh into 1 cm (½ inch) cubes, then use a spoon to scoop out the remaining flesh from the skin and put it in a bowl.

3 Add the onion, chillies and coriander to the bowl and mix together gently, making sure that you don't squash the avocado. Add a little lime juice to taste and season to taste with salt. Garnish with coriander leaves and serve immediately with the totopos.

# VEGETABLE KEBABS WITH PILAF

**1** In a large bowl combine the rosemary with 2 tablespoons oil and salt and pepper. Cut the courgettes and red pepper into large pieces, add to the oil with the mushrooms and tomatoes and toss well. Cover and leave to marinate for 20 minutes.

**2** Wash the rice under cold water, drain and put in a saucepan. Add lightly salted water to cover the rice by at least 5 cm (2 inches). Bring to the boil and boil for 10 minutes. Drain well.

**3** Heat the remaining oil in a separate saucepan, add the onion, garlic and cardamom pods and cook over a medium heat, stirring frequently, for 5 minutes until lightly golden. Add the rice, cranberries, pistachios and coriander. Season to taste with salt and pepper. Stir well, remove from the heat, cover and leave to rest for 10 minutes.

**4** Meanwhile, thread the vegetables alternately on to eight pre-soaked wooden skewers. Cook on a medium-hot barbecue, turning frequently, for 10 minutes until all the vegetables are tender. Serve with the rice and Greek-style yogurt.

1 tablespoon chopped rosemary
5 tablespoons extra virgin olive oil
2 courgettes
1 large red pepper, cored and deseeded
16 button mushrooms, trimmed
8 cherry tomatoes
Greek-style yogurt, to serve

**Pilaf**
250 g (8 oz) basmati rice
1 onion, finely chopped
2 garlic cloves, finely chopped
6 cardamom pods, bruised
100 g (3½ oz) dried cranberries
50 g (2 oz) pistachios, toasted and chopped
2 tablespoons chopped fresh coriander
salt and pepper

Serves **4**
Prep time **20 minutes, plus marinating and resting**
Cooking time **20 minutes**

# **NASI** GORENG

*A QUICK AND TASTY SUMMER SUPPER TO ENJOY IN THE SUN AND REMIND YOU OF YOUR GAP YEAR TREKKING ACROSS INDONESIA.*

**1** Heat the oil in a wok or large frying pan, add the chicken and stir-fry for 1 minute. Add the shrimps, garlic, carrot and cabbage and stir-fry for 3-4 minutes.

**2** Pour in the egg spread it with a wooden spoon. Cook until set, then break it up. Add the rice and stir to mix.

**3** Add the soy sauce, sesame oil and chilli sauce and heat through. Serve immediately, garnished with chilli strips.

2 tablespoons vegetable oil
150 g (5 oz) boneless, skinless chicken breast, finely chopped
50 g (2 oz) cooked peeled shrimps (thawed if frozen)
1 garlic clove, crushed
1 carrot, grated
¼ white cabbage, thinly sliced
1 egg, beaten
300 g (10 oz) cold cooked basmati rice
2 tablespoons sweet soy sauce (kecap manis)
½ teaspoon sesame oil
1 tablespoon chilli sauce
1 red chilli, deseeded and cut into strips, to garnish

**Serves 4**
**Prep time 10 minutes**
**Cooking time 10 minutes**

AFFORDABILITY
3

**AFFORDABILITY 1**

# CHEESY GARLIC BREAD

1 Cut 20 slices in the French stick without going all the way through. Combine the oil, garlic, thyme and salt and pepper in a bowl and brush the mixture all over the cut sides and the top of the bread.

2 Put a slice of mozzarella between each slice of bread, place the stick on a double layer of kitchen foil and seal loosely. Cook on a medium-hot barbecue for 5 minutes, then open out the foil (using oven gloves because the foil will be hot) and cook for a further 5 minutes. Serve hot.

1 small French stick
75 ml (3 fl oz) extra virgin olive oil
1 garlic clove, crushed
2 teaspoons chopped thyme
125 g (4 oz) buffalo mozzarella cheese, thinly sliced
salt and black pepper

Serves **4**
Prep time **5 minutes**
Cooking time **10 minutes**

# CAESAR SALAD

1 garlic clove, crushed
4 anchovy fillets, chopped
4 tablespoons lemon juice
2 teaspoons dry English
  mustard
1 egg yolk
200 ml (7 fl oz) extra virgin
  olive oil
vegetable oil, for frying
3 slices of country bread, cubed
1 cos lettuce, washed and torn
  into pieces
3 tablespoons grated Parmesan
  cheese
pepper

Serves 4
Prep time **20 minutes**
Cooking time **5 minutes**

**1** Put the garlic, anchovy fillets, lemon juice, mustard and egg yolk in a small mixing bowl and season with pepper. Use a hand-held blender or small whisk to mix well until combined. Drizzle in the olive oil, mixing all the time, to make a thick, creamy sauce. If the sauce becomes too thick, add a little water.

**2** Heat the vegetable oil in a frying pan. Test with a small piece of bread to see if it is hot enough; if the bread sizzles, add the bread cubes, turning them when they are golden. When they are cooked, transfer them to a plate lined with kitchen paper to absorb the excess oil.

**3** Put the lettuce in a large bowl, pour over the dressing and 2 tablespoons grated Parmesan and mix well.

**4** Serve the salad in a large bowl or on individual plates, sprinkled with the croutons and the remaining Parmesan.

AFFORDABILITY
2

# TOMATO & GREEN BEAN SALAD

**AFFORDABILITY 1**

1 Cut the tomatoes into halves and put them into a large bowl.

2 Cook the green beans in boiling water for 2 minutes, drain well and place in the bowl with the tomatoes.

3 Add the mint, garlic, oil and vinegar. Season to taste with salt and pepper and mix well. Serve warm or cold.

250 g (8 oz) baby red tomatoes (plum if possible)
250 g (8 oz) thin green beans, topped and tailed
handful of mint, chopped
1 garlic clove, crushed and chopped
4 tablespoons extra virgin olive oil
1 tablespoon balsamic vinegar
salt and pepper

**Serves 4**
**Prep time 10 minutes**
**Cooking time 2 minutes**

# GREEK-STYLE
# FETA
# SALAD

4 tomatoes, cut into wedges
½ cucumber, cut into bite-sized
  cubes
1 red pepper, cored, deseeded
  and cut into rings or thinly
  sliced
1 red onion, thinly sliced
200 g (7 oz) feta cheese, cubed
100 g (3½ oz) pitted black olives
4 tablespoons olive oil
2 tablespoons white wine
  vinegar
2-3 teaspoons finely chopped
  oregano
salt and pepper

Serves **4**
Prep time **15 minutes**

**1** Arrange the tomatoes, cucumber, green pepper and onion in
a serving dish.

**2** Scatter the cheese and olives over the salad, season well
with salt and pepper and drizzle with the oil and vinegar.
Sprinkle over the oregano before serving.

# COLESLAW

½ white cabbage
¼ red cabbage
2 carrots
1 red onion
2 tablespoons roughly chopped
   parsley

**Dressing**
300 ml (½ pint) mayonnaise
1 tablespoon white wine vinegar
½ teaspoon caster sugar
salt and pepper

Serves **4**
Prep time **15 minutes, plus
standing**

**1** Finely shred both cabbages and the carrots and finely slice
the onion. Mix the cabbages and carrots in a large salad
bowl with the onion and add the parsley.

**2** Make the dressing by whisking together the mayonnaise,
vinegar and sugar. Season to taste with salt and pepper.
Toss the dressing through the cabbage mixture, then leave to
stand for at least 30 minutes before serving.

AFFORDABILITY
**1**

# POTATO SALAD

**1** Halve the potatoes and cook in lightly salted boiling water until tender. Rinse under cold water and leave to cool.

**2** Meanwhile, cut the bacon into thin strips. Heat the oil in a frying pan, add the bacon and cook until golden. Drain on kitchen paper and allow to cool. Finely slice the spring onions, reserving some for garnish.

**3** Put the potatoes, finely sliced spring onions and bacon in a large salad bowl. Gently stir in the mayonnaise. Season to taste with salt and pepper, garnish with the reserved spring onions and serve.

1 kg (2 lb) new potatoes
125 g (4 oz) smoked streaky bacon
1 teaspoon vegetable oil
6 spring onions
175 ml (6 fl oz) mayonnaise
salt and pepper

**Serves 4-6**
**Prep time 10 minutes, plus cooling**
**Cooking time 15 minutes**

# PANZANELLA

3 red peppers, cored, deseeded
   and quartered
375 g (12 oz) ripe plum
   tomatoes, skinned
6 tablespoons extra virgin olive
   oil
3 tablespoons wine vinegar
2 garlic cloves, crushed
125 g (4 oz) stale ciabatta bread
50 g (2 oz) pitted black olives
small handful of basil leaves,
   shredded
salt and pepper

Serves **4**
Prep time **15 minutes**
Cooking time **10 minutes**

1 Put the peppers, skin side up, on a foil-lined grill rack and grill under a preheated moderate grill for 10 minutes or until the skins are blackened.

2 Meanwhile, quarter the tomatoes and scoop out the pulp, placing it in a sieve over a bowl to catch the juices. Set the tomato quarters aside. Press the pulp with the back of a spoon to extract as much juice as possible. Beat the oil, vinegar, garlic and salt and pepper into the tomato juice.

3 When they are cool enough to handle, peel the skins from the peppers and discard. Roughly slice the peppers and place in a bowl with the tomato quarters. Break the bread into small chunks and add to the bowl with the olives and basil.

4 Add the dressing and toss the ingredients together before serving.

# WARM **COURGETTE** *&* **LIME** SALAD

IF YOU PREFER, YOU CAN COOK THIN SLICES OF
AUBERGINE IN THE SAME WAY.

1 Put the oil, lime rind and juice, garlic, coriander and a little salt and pepper in a polythene bag. Add the courgettes and shake gently in the bag to coat. Seal and set aside until ready to cook.

2 Heat a ridged frying pan until smoking. Arrange as many courgette slices as will fit in a single layer over the base of the pan and cook for 2-3 minutes until the undersides are browned. Turn the courgettes over and brown on the other side, then transfer to a warmed serving dish while you cook the remainder.

3 Pour any remaining dressing over the courgettes, sprinkle with chopped coriander to garnish and serve immediately.

1 tablespoon olive oil
finely grated rind and juice of
  1 lime
1 garlic clove, finely chopped
2 tablespoons roughly
  chopped fresh coriander
  leaves, plus extra to garnish
2 courgettes, about 325 g
  (11 oz) in total, cut into thin
  diagonal slices
salt and pepper

Serves 4
Prep time **10 minutes**
Cooking time **8 minutes**

4 small wheat tortillas
1 tablespoon olive oil

**Hummus**
410 g (13½ oz) can chickpeas,
  rinsed and drained
1 garlic clove, chopped
4–6 tablespoons natural yogurt
2 tablespoons lemon juice
1 tablespoon chopped fresh
  coriander leaves
salt and pepper
paprika, to sprinkle

**To serve**
lemon wedges
olives

Serves 4
Prep time **5 minutes**
Cooking time **10-12 minutes**

# BAKED
# TORTILLAS
## *WITH* HUMMUS

**1** Cut each tortilla into 8 triangles, put them on a baking sheet and brush with a little oil. Cook in a preheated oven, 200ºC (400ºF), Gas Mark 6, for 10-12 minutes, until golden and crisp. Remove from the oven.

**2** Meanwhile, put the chickpeas, garlic, yogurt and lemon juice in a bowl and mix thoroughly until smooth. Sprinkle with salt and pepper, stir in the coriander and sprinkle with paprika. Serve with the warm tortillas, lemon wedges and olives.

# FALAFEL
## *cakes*

AFFORDABILITY 1

AS WELL AS MAKING A TASTY, HEALTHY TEA, THESE
ARE A GREAT ADDITION TO ANY PICNIC WHEN
SERVED WITH HUMMUS (SEE OPPOSITE).

**1** Put the chickpeas in a food processor or blender with the onion, garlic, spices, herbs, breadcrumbs and a little salt and pepper. Blend briefly to make a chunky paste.

**2** Take dessertspoonfuls of the mixture and flatten into cakes. Add oil to a frying pan to a depth of 1 cm (½ inch), heat and fry half the falafel for about 3 minutes, turning once, until crisp and golden. Drain on kitchen paper and keep warm while you cook the remainder.

400 g (13 oz) can chickpeas, rinsed and drained
1 onion, roughly chopped
3 garlic cloves, roughly chopped
2 teaspoons cumin seeds
1 teaspoon mild chilli powder
2 tablespoons chopped mint
3 tablespoons chopped fresh coriander
50 g (2 oz) fresh breadcrumbs
oil, for shallow-frying
salt and pepper

Serves **4**
Prep time **10 minutes**
Cooking time **10 minutes**

# ORANGE SUPER-SMOOTHIE

1 large carrot
1 orange
100 g (3½ oz) banana
1 fresh or dried apricot
2-3 ice cubes

Serves 1
Prep time **5 minutes**

1 Peel the carrot and orange and juice the two together. If you are using a blender, chop into smaller pieces.

2 Transfer the juice to a food processor or blender, add the banana, apricot and a couple of ice cubes and blend briefly.

3 Pour the smoothie into a glass and serve immediately.

AFFORDABILITY
1

# BANANA & PEANUT BUTTER SMOOTHIE

THIS IS TASTY ENOUGH TO SATISFY EVERYONE'S SWEET CRAVINGS (AND SAVE YOU THE LONG QUEUES AT THE ICE CREAM VAN).

1 ripe banana
300 ml (½ pint) semi-skimmed milk
1 tablespoon smooth peanut butter or 2 teaspoons tahini paste

Serves 2
Prep time **5 minutes, plus freezing**

1 Peel and slice the banana, put it in a freezer container and freeze for at least 2 hours or overnight.

2 Put the banana, milk and peanut butter or tahini paste in a food processor or blender and process until smooth.

3 Pour the smoothie into a tall glass. Serve immediately.

AFFORDABILITY
1

AFFORDABILITY
1

# STRAWBERRY LASSI

REFRESHING AND PACKED WITH VITAMIN C, THIS MAKES A GREAT
ALTERNATIVE TO DRINKING BEERS ALL DAY IN THE PARK.

1 Put the strawberries in a food processor with half the cold
water. Blend until smooth.

2 Add the yogurt, sugar, remaining water and the rosewater
and blitz until smooth and frothy. Pour into chilled, tall
glasses, sprinkle with black pepper and serve immediately.

400 g (13 oz) strawberries,
  hulled and roughly chopped
300 ml (½ pint) low-fat natural
  yogurt
25 g (1 oz) golden caster sugar
750 ml (1¼ pints) ice cold water
few drops of rosewater
coarsely ground black pepper,
  to serve

**Serves 4**
**Prep time 10 minutes**

74  CHICKEN FAJITAS

75  SPANISH MARINADE WITH CHICKEN

76  SUCCULENT ROAST CHICKEN

78  BAKED TURKEY BURRITO

79  TURKEY WITH CREOLE SAUCE

80  CRISPY DUCK LEGS WITH MINI ROAST POTATOES

81  POT-ROASTED PORK WITH LENTILS

84  PORK STEAKS WITH APPLES & MUSTARD MASH

85  SWEET & SOUR PORK

86  BEEF STROGANOFF

87  STEAK & MUSHROOM PIE

88  MOUSSAKA

89  STUFFED AUBERGINES

90  FISH PIE

92  SEAFOOD PAELLA

93  PAD THAI

94  CHILLI PRAWNS WITH GARLIC & SPINACH

95  SALMON FISHCAKES WITH SPINACH & POACHED EGGS

96  GRILLED HADDOCK WITH LENTILS & SPINACH

97  CREAMY FISH LASAGNE

98  CHERRY TOMATO & RICOTTA PENNE

99  RIBBON PASTA WITH AUBERGINE & PINE NUTS

100  CHERRY TOMATO TARTS WITH PESTO CREME FRAICHE

101  MUSHROOM & BROCCOLI PIE

102  VEGETABLE BOLOGNESE

103  SPINACH, ONION & CREAM CHEESE PIZZA

104  PIZZA FIORENTINA

105  PIZZA PUFF PIES

106  GRILLED COURGETTES WITH GOATS' CHEESE

108  PESTO ALLA GENOVESE

109  ROAST POTATOES WITH ROSEMARY & GARLIC

110  PATATAS BRAVAS

111  GRILLED VEGETABLE & HALOUMI SALAD

112  MINT & LEMON GRASS TEA

113  GREEN TEA

PESTO ALLA GENOVESE

GRILLED VEGETABLE
& HALOUMI SALAD

# MATES
# FOR TEA

TURKEY WITH CREOLE SAUCE

# CHICKEN FAJITAS

1 tablespoon olive oil
1 large red onion, thinly sliced
1 red pepper, cored, deseeded and
  thinly sliced
1 yellow pepper, cored, deseeded
  and thinly sliced
450 g (14½ oz) boneless, skinless
  chicken breasts, cut into thin
  strips
⅛ teaspoon paprika
⅛ teaspoon mild chilli powder
⅛ teaspoon ground cumin
¼ teaspoon dried oregano
4 soft flour tortillas
½ iceberg lettuce, finely shredded
guacamole, to serve (optional)

**Tomato salsa**

1 small red onion, finely chopped
425 g (14 oz) small vine-ripened
  tomatoes
2 garlic cloves, crushed
large handful of fresh coriander
  leaves, chopped
pepper

Serves **4**
Prep time **15 minutes, plus
chilling**
Cooking time **10 minutes**

1 Prepare the tomato salsa. In a small bowl mix together the chopped onion, tomatoes, garlic and coriander. Season with pepper, cover and chill for 30 minutes to allow the flavours to develop.

2 Heat the oil in a wok or large, nonstick frying pan, add the onion and peppers and cook for 3–4 minutes. Add the chicken, paprika, chilli powder, cumin and oregano and stir-fry for 5 minutes until the chicken is cooked through.

3 Meanwhile, wrap the tortillas in kitchen foil and warm them in the oven for 5 minutes or according to the pack instructions.

4 Spoon one-quarter of the chicken mixture into the centre of each tortilla and add a couple of tablespoons of the salsa and some shredded lettuce. Roll up and serve warm, accompanied by guacamole, if liked.

AFFORDABILITY
2

### Chops away

For the price of a round of happy-hour drinks, you can invest in a mini food processor. They make short work of chopping onions, garlic, chillies and other ingredients, saving you valuable drinking time and avoiding close contact with sharp knives.

# SPANISH MARINADE
## WITH CHICKEN

1 Make the marinade. Mix together all the ingredients and season to taste with salt and pepper. Rub the marinade thoroughly into the skin of the chicken. Drizzle the olive oil over the chicken and leave to marinate in the refrigerator for at least 2 hours, but preferably overnight.

2 Transfer the chicken to a roasting tray and cook in a preheated oven, 180°C (350°F), Gas Mark 4, for 1½ hours.

3 Put the chicken on a warm plate, cover with kitchen foil and leave to rest in a warm place for about 10 minutes before carving.

1 large chicken, about 1.8 kg (4 lb)
4 tablespoons Spanish extra virgin olive oil

**Marinade**
250 ml (8 fl oz) full-fat natural yogurt
1 teaspoon smoked paprika
grated rind and juice of 1 lemon
1 tablespoon red wine vinegar
1 small onion, finely grated
2 garlic cloves, crushed
2 tablespoons chopped parsley, plus extra for serving
salt and pepper

Serves **4**
Prep time **12 minutes, plus marinating and resting**
Cooking time **1½ hours**

# SUCCULENT
# ROAST CHICKEN

150 g (5 oz) soft goats' cheese
1 hot red chilli, deseeded and
chopped
25 g (1 oz) prosciutto, chopped
3 garlic cloves, crushed
2 teaspoons chopped
rosemary, plus several extra
sprigs
small handful flat leaf parsley,
chopped
1.5 kg (3 lb) chicken
50 g (2 oz) butter, softened
1 large glass of white wine
salt

Serves **5-6**
Prep time **20 minutes**
Cooking time **1½ hours**

PACKING STUFFING UNDER THE SKIN OF A CHICKEN
IS THE BEST WAY TO LET THE DELICIOUS FLAVOURS
PENETRATE THE MEAT. IT ALSO SEEPS RIGHT
THROUGH TO THE JUICES FOR THE GRAVY.

1 Mix together the cheese, chilli, prosciutto, garlic, chopped
rosemary, parsley and a little salt.

2 Slide your fingers between the chicken breast and skin,
then push a little further under the skin to release the skin
from the tops of the leg joints. Use a teaspoon to pack the
cheese mixture between the skin and the meat. Smooth the skin
back into place, at the same time spreading the stuffing in an
even layer.

3 So that the chicken keeps its shape during cooking it's
usual to truss the bird before cooking it. Take a long piece
of kitchen string and put the chicken on a board with the legs
towards you. Centre the twine under the legs, pass it over the
legs and pull the ends so that the legs cross and are held
securely together. Wind the ends once round the legs and then
take them down the sides so that the wings are pressed against
the body. Turn over the bird and make sure the flap of skin at
the neck end is tucked neatly into the aperture. Fasten the
string in a bow (for easy removal).

4 Sit the chicken over the extra rosemary sprigs in a
roasting tin and spread with the butter. Roast in a
preheated oven, 190°C (375°F), Gas Mark 5, for 1½ hours or
until the juices run clear when the thigh is pierced with a skewer.

5 Drain to a serving plate and leave to stand in a warm place
for 15 minutes. Add the wine to the roasting tin, stirring to
scrape up the residue, and allow it to bubble for a few minutes.
Check the seasoning and serve with the chicken.

**AFFORDABILITY**

**3**

## Jointing a chicken

It's cheaper to buy a whole chicken and joint it yourself than to buy separate portions. Using a really sharp knife, cut down the length of the back of the chicken, then open it out flat on to the chopping board and cut through the breast bone, so you now have two halves. Cut along the natural line of skin to separate the legs from the breasts and cut the legs from the thighs if you need six portions. Easy!

# BAKED **TURKEY** BURRITO

4 tablespoons vegetable oil
500 g (1 lb) turkey breast, thinly sliced
1 large onion, sliced
1 red pepper, cored, deseeded and sliced
1 yellow pepper, cored, deseeded and sliced
150 g (5 oz) can red kidney beans, rinsed and drained
150 g (5 oz) cooked rice
juice of 1 lime
8 plain flour tortillas
6 tablespoons medium-hot salsa
2 tablespoons sliced preserved jalapeño peppers (optional)
250 g (8 oz) Cheddar cheese, grated
salt and pepper

**To serve**
guacamole
½ iceberg lettuce, shredded

Serves **4**
Prep time **12 minutes**
Cooking time **30-33 minutes**

1 Heat 2 tablespoons oil in a large frying pan and stir-fry the sliced turkey for 3-4 minutes until it is beginning to colour. Remove it with a slotted spoon. Increase the heat, add the remaining oil and fry the onion and peppers for 5-6 minutes, stirring only occasionally so that they colour quickly without softening too much.

2 Reduce the heat, return the turkey to the pan and stir in the beans and cooked rice. Season well, squeeze over the lime juice and remove from the heat. Spoon the filling on to the tortillas, roll them up and arrange them in a single layer in a rectangular ovenproof dish.

3 Pour the salsa over the tortillas and scatter over the jalapeño peppers (if used) and cheese. Cook in a preheated oven, 200°C (400°F), Gas Mark 6, for about 20 minutes until hot and the cheese has melted. Serve immediately with guacamole and shredded lettuce.

# TURKEY WITH CREOLE SAUCE

FRYING TURKEY PIECES IN A CRISP, SPICY CRUMB COATING KEEPS THE MEAT MOIST AND SUCCULENT. THE PINEAPPLE AND PEPPER SAUCE ADDS A DELICIOUS CONTRAST IN BOTH TEXTURE AND FLAVOUR.

1 Cut the turkey across into 1 cm (½ inch) thick slices, then cut each slice into 1 cm (½ inch) strips. Mix the paprika, flour and a little salt and coat the turkey in the mixture. Dip the turkey in the beaten egg and then in the breadcrumbs until coated.

2 Make the sauce. Heat the oil in a sauté pan or large frying pan and gently fry the onion and peppers for 5-8 minutes until softened. Add the garlic, tomatoes, pineapple, Tabasco sauce and a little salt to the pan and cook gently, stirring frequently, for about 10 minutes or until pulpy. If the pineapple isn't very sweet add a little sugar to the sauce.

3 Heat 1 cm (½ inch) of oil in a pan until a few breadcrumbs gently sizzle. Fry half the turkey pieces in the oil until golden, turning once. Drain on kitchen paper while you cook the rest. Serve with the sauce.

500 g (1 lb) turkey breast fillet
½ teaspoon paprika
1 tablespoon plain flour
1 egg, beaten
100 g (3½ oz) fresh breadcrumbs
vegetable oil, for frying
salt

**Creole sauce**
2 tablespoons vegetable oil
1 onion, chopped
2 red peppers, cored, deseeded
  and chopped
2 garlic cloves, crushed
500 g (1 lb) tomatoes, skinned and
  chopped
1 small, sweet pineapple, skinned,
  cored and chopped
2 teaspoons Tabasco sauce

Serves **4**
Prep time **25 minutes**
Cooking time **25 minutes**

AFFORDABILITY
1

# CRISPY
## DUCK LEGS
## WITH MINI
## ROAST POTATOES

AFFORDABILITY
2

4 duck legs
1 tablespoon chopped thyme
2 teaspoons sea salt
½ teaspoon pepper
8 tablespoons extra virgin olive oil
1 frisée lettuce

**Mini roast potatoes**
3 tablespoons extra virgin olive oil
2–3 thyme sprigs
750 g (1½ lb) floury potatoes, cubed
4 garlic cloves
salt and pepper

**Dressing**
3 tablespoons extra virgin olive oil
1 tablespoon shallot vinegar
1 shallot, preferably purple, very finely diced
¼ teaspoon Dijon mustard
pinch of sugar

Serves **4**
Prep time **10 minutes, plus marinating**
Cooking time **1½ hours**

IN THIS MODERN TWIST ON THE CLASSIC ROAST, THE CRISP SKIN OF THE POTATOES COMPLEMENTS THE RICH DUCK MEAT, WHICH IS GENTLY FLAVOURED BY THE THYME.

1 Rub the duck legs in the thyme, salt and pepper, cover and leave at room temperature for about 1 hour.

2 Heat the olive oil in a shallow flameproof casserole and place the duck legs, flesh side down, in the oil. Cook in a preheated oven, 190°C (375°F), Gas Mark 5, for about 1½ hours, basting occasionally, until the flesh is tender.

3 Prepare the roast potatoes. Put the olive oil and thyme sprigs in a bowl and season well with salt and pepper. Add the potatoes and garlic and toss well. Tip them into a roasting tin and roast alongside the duck for about 45 minutes until they are golden and crispy.

4 Whisk together the dressing ingredients, toss with the lettuce to coat well with dressing and serve with the crispy duck and potatoes.

# POT-ROASTED PORK *with* LENTILS

1 Cook the lentils in boiling water for 20 minutes. Drain and set aside.

2 Season the meat on all sides. Melt the butter with the oil in a large, heavy-based frying pan and sear the meat on all sides until it is browned. Transfer the pork to a large casserole dish.

3 Add the onions to the pan and fry for 5 minutes. Add the garlic and rosemary sprigs and cook for 1 minute. Tip the onion and herbs into the casserole dish and cover with a lid. Roast in a preheated oven, 180°C (350°F), Gas Mark 4, for 1¼ hours.

4 Tip the lentils around the meat and add the capers, anchovies, wine and seasoning. Return to the oven for a further 30 minutes, then leave to stand for 15 minutes before carving.

225 g (7½ oz) Puy lentils, rinsed
1.5 kg (3 lb) joint of pork (loin or chump end), skinned, boned and rolled
50 g (2 oz) butter
2 tablespoons olive oil
2 onions, sliced
4 garlic cloves, crushed
several rosemary sprigs
2 tablespoons capers, rinsed and drained
5 anchovy fillets, chopped
200 ml (7 fl oz) white wine
salt and pepper

Serves **6**
Prep time **20 minutes, plus standing**
Cooking time **2 hours**

## Cooked meat

Don't let food poisoning add to the number of duvet days you take during term time. When it comes to cooking meat, you can't take any chances, so always follow the cooking instructions exactly. To make sure your meat is cooked through, push a skewer or sharp, thin-bladed knife into the thickest part – if the juices run clear, you're in the clear; if they're pink, the meat needs more cooking time.

# LET ME
## ENTERTAIN
# YOU

If your idea of a dinner party is a Chinese take-away and as many beers as you can carry from the off-licence, think again. With forward planning you can create an ambience and menu to mark you out as the 'sophisticated student'.

## PLAN AHEAD

Every good host(ess) will tell you that a successful dinner party relies almost entirely on good planning (burned food, power cuts or food poisoning could obviously put a bit of damper on proceedings, but let's assume they're off the menu). It's true that you probably don't have the budget, time or home entertaining skills (no offence) to throw a bash worthy of note in a food magazine, but if you plan ahead and make lots of lists there's less potential for disaster. Decide on your menu a week in advance to allow time to shop according to your means, and give people plenty of notice about the date – although this isn't quite as important as most students would miss the Second Coming for a free meal.

## COUNT YOUR CUTLERY

There's nothing worse than being found wanting on the crockery and cutlery front. Although you could substitute paper plates for porcelain at a push, no one wants to eat mash or pasta with their fingers. Check you have enough knives, forks, plates and glasses a day or two before and borrow extras if you need to.

## BRING A BOTTLE

It's all very well you making the effort to cook for your mates, but you shouldn't have to supply all the booze as well. Make it clear that your guests should bring a bottle of whatever they fancy drinking or you could be left hosting a dry dinner party. There are always a few who – if left unprompted – will arrive holding nothing more than their coat and spend the night drinking everyone else's alcohol.

## KEEP IT SIMPLE

Don't try to cook beyond your capabilities. Plan an easy menu that you know you can prepare without giving yourself a nervous breakdown. A simple, cold starter (such as Caesar Salad, page 60) is ideal because you can prepare it ahead. Or just serve warm crusty bread and some good-quality ham and olives. Choose a main course that is easy to prepare, cook and serve – one-pot meals are perfect – and for pudding either ask a friend to make something or stick to a simple 'assembly job'.

# PORK STEAKS
## WITH APPLES
### & MUSTARD MASH

AFFORDABILITY
2

4 floury potatoes, peeled and
  diced
1 large green apple, peeled, cored
  and quartered
handful of sage leaves, chopped
2 tablespoons extra virgin olive oil
1 tablespoon lemon juice
1 tablespoon clear honey
4 pork steaks, about 200 g (7 oz)
  each
50 g (2 oz) butter
2 tablespoons milk
1 tablespoon Dijon mustard
salt and pepper

Serves **4**
Prep time **5 minutes**
Cooking time **23 minutes**

1 Cook the potatoes in a saucepan of lightly salted boiling
  water for 10 minutes, until tender.

2 Cut the apple quarters into thick wedges. Mix the
  sage with the oil, lemon juice and honey and season
to taste with salt and pepper. Mix half the flavoured oil
with the apple wedges and brush the remainder over the
pork steaks.

3 Cook the steaks under a hot grill for 3-4 minutes on each
  side, until browned and cooked through. Set aside and
keep warm.

4 Drain the potatoes, mash and beat in 40 g (1½ oz) butter,
  the milk and mustard and season to taste with salt and
pepper. Keep warm.

5 Melt the remaining butter in a frying pan and quickly fry
  the apple wedges for 2-3 minutes or until golden and
softened. Serve the pork with the mustard mash, apples
and any pork juices.

# SWEET & SOUR
# PORK

1 Mix together the egg white and pepper and coat the pork slices in the mixture. Dip each piece of pork into the cornflour, shaking off the excess.

2 Heat the oil in a large, nonstick frying pan over a high heat until piping hot, add the pork slices, making sure there is a little space between each one and fry for 2 minutes on each side. Turn down the heat to medium and stir-fry the pork for another 2 minutes or until done. Transfer to a serving plate and keep warm.

3 Make the cornflour paste. Mix the cornflour with the water or stock to make a smooth paste without any lumps.

4 Make the sweet and sour sauce. Combine all the ingredients in a small saucepan, bring to the boil and thicken with the cornflour paste. Pour the sauce over the pork and serve with rice, if liked.

1 egg white, slightly beaten
1 teaspoon black pepper
500 g (1 lb) pork fillet or loin, cut
    into 1 cm (½ inch) thick slices
4 tablespoons cornflour
1 tablespoon rapeseed or olive oil

**Cornflour paste**
5 teaspoons cornflour
5 tablespoons stock or water

**Sweet and sour sauce**
3 tablespoons tomato ketchup
1 teaspoon white wine vinegar
200 g (7 oz) tomatoes, roughly
    chopped
4 tablespoons pineapple juice
2 teaspoons sugar
200 ml (7 fl oz) water
150 g (5 oz) pineapple pieces
150 g (5 oz) green pepper, cored,
    deseeded and cut into 2.5 cm
    (1 inch) pieces
125 g (4 oz) onion, cut into 2.5 cm
    (1 inch) pieces
4 tablespoons lemon juice

Serves **2**
Prep time **20 minutes**
Cooking time **10 minutes**

AFFORDABILITY
2

## Keep your cloths clean

Admit it – you use the kitchen cloth for everything from mopping up milk to cleaning your bike chain. Damp, dirty kitchen cloths are a natural paradise for germs – a good way to zap germs is give cloths a rinse and a good squeeze, put them flat in the microwave and turn up the power for 2–3 minutes.

# BEEF *STROGANOFF*

50 g (2 oz) butter
3 onions, finely chopped
250 g (8 oz) button mushrooms, thinly sliced
1 green pepper, cored, deseeded and cut into fine strips
500 g (1 lb) fillet steak or good rump steak, cut into strips 5 cm (2 in) long and 5 mm (¼ inch) thick
150 ml (¼ pint) soured cream
salt and pepper
1 teaspoon chopped parsley, to garnish

1 Melt half the butter in a large, deep frying pan and fry the onions until pale golden. Add the mushrooms and green pepper to the pan and cook for 5 minutes. Remove the onions, mushrooms and green pepper from the pan.

2 Add the remaining butter, allow it to become hot, then fry the steak strips for about 4 minutes, turning so they are cooked evenly.

3 Return the onions, mushrooms and peppers to the pan and season well, then stir in the soured cream and blend well. Heat until piping hot, but do not allow to boil. Garnish with chopped parsley before serving.

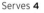

Serves **4**
Prep time **10 minutes**
Cooking time **15 minutes**

AFFORDABILITY
3

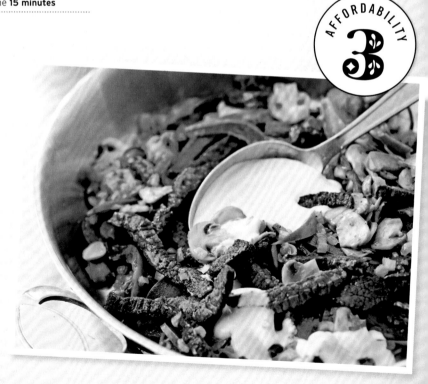

# STEAK & MUSHROOM PIE

1 Season the flour and use it to coat the steak. Heat a dot of butter in a large, heavy-based frying pan and fry the meat in batches until it is well browned, using a slotted spoon to drain and transfer each batch to an ovenproof casserole dish. Gently fry the onion and garlic in a little more butter until softened.

2 Add the stout, stock, bay leaves, horseradish sauce and a little seasoning to the frying pan. Bring to the boil and pour the mixture over the meat. Transfer to a preheated oven, 150°C (300°F), Gas Mark 2, and cook for 1½ hours until the meat is tender.

3 Meanwhile, fry the mushrooms in the remaining butter for 5 minutes and add them to the beef for the last 30 minutes of the cooking time. Leave to cool, then turn the meat mixture into a 1 litre (1¾ pint) pie dish and chill.

4 Roll out the pastry until it is 5 cm (2 inches) larger than the dish and use it to cover the pie. Bake in a preheated oven, 190°C (375°F), Gas Mark 5, for 45 minutes until deep golden.

3 tablespoons plain flour
750 g (1½ lb) stewing steak, diced
50 g (2 oz) butter
1 large onion, chopped
2 garlic cloves, crushed
450 ml (¾ pint) stout
150 ml (¼ pint) Beef Stock (see page 234)
2 bay leaves
1 tablespoon hot horseradish sauce
250 g (8 oz) cup mushrooms
275 g (9 oz) shortcrust pastry (thawed if frozen)
milk, to glaze
salt and pepper

Serves **4**
Prep time **40 minutes, plus cooling**
Cooking time **2½ hours**

## Spotless microwave

It's a dirty job, but someone's got to do it. Here's an easy way: put some lemon slices in a bowl of water and microwave on high until the water is boiling (3–4 minutes). The steam will loosen the built-up grime and most of it should be easy to wipe off with a damp cloth. The bonus is your kitchen will smell nice too.

# MOUSSAKA

BRUSHING THE AUBERGINES WITH OIL AND GRILLING RATHER THAN FRYING THEM GIVES A LIGHTER, LESS 'FATTY-TASTING' DISH. THE TANGY FETA TOPPING IS ALSO LOVELY AND LIGHT, BUT YOU CAN USE A MORE SUBSTANTIAL CHEESE, SUCH AS GRUYÈRE OR CHEDDAR, IF YOU PREFER.

500 g (1 lb) aubergines
8 tablespoons oil
1 large onion, finely chopped
500 g (1 lb) lean minced lamb
400 g (13 oz) can chopped
   tomatoes
1 teaspoon dried oregano
4 garlic cloves, crushed
150 ml (¼ pint) red wine
300 ml (½ pint) Greek-style
   yogurt
2 eggs, beaten
100 g (3½ oz) feta cheese,
   crumbled
salt and pepper

Serves **4**
Prep time **25 minutes**
Cooking time **1½ hours**

1 Cut the aubergines into thin slices and arrange them in a single layer on a foil-lined grill rack. Blend 5 tablespoons oil with plenty of salt and pepper and brush a little over the aubergines. Grill until golden, then turn and grill again, brushing with more oil. (If necessary, grill in two batches.)

2 Heat the remaining oil in a large, heavy-based saucepan and fry the onion and lamb for 10 minutes until browned. Stir in the tomatoes, oregano, garlic, wine and a little seasoning. Cover and cook gently for 20 minutes or until pulpy.

3 Spread a quarter of the meat sauce in the base of a shallow, 2 litre (3½ pint) ovenproof dish and cover with one-third of the aubergine slices. Repeat layering, finishing with the meat sauce.

4 Beat together the yogurt and eggs and spoon over the meat. Crumble over the feta and bake in a preheated oven, 180°C (350°F), Gas Mark 4, for about 45 minutes until the topping is golden.

# STUFFED
# AUBERGINES

AFFORDABILITY
2

1 Rinse and dry the aubergines. Cut them in half lengthways and hollow out some of the flesh with a small spoon. Place the shells in a baking dish in a preheated oven, 180°C (350°F), Gas Mark 5, for around 10 minutes.

2 Season the minced lamb with the cinnamon and with a little salt and pepper.

3 Heat the oil in a nonstick saucepan, add the onion and cook until golden. Add the lamb, rice, pine nuts, mint and chopped parsley and mix well.

4 Fill the aubergine shells with this mixture and return to the oven for around 15 minutes. If necessary, add a little water in the bottom of the dish to make sure they do not stick. Serve warm or cold.

4 aubergines
300 g (10 oz) minced lamb
2 pinches of ground cinnamon
1 tablespoon olive oil
1 onion, chopped
80 g (3 oz) cooked long grain rice
20 g (¾ oz) pine nuts
2 tablespoons finely chopped mint leaves
2 tablespoons finely chopped parsley
salt and pepper

Serves **4**
Prep time **30 minutes**
Cooking time **25 minutes**

# FISH PIE

A GOOD FISH PIE IS A CLASSIC, COMFORTING DISH THAT NEVER GOES OUT OF FASHION.

1 kg (2 lb) cod fillet, skinned
3 tablespoons milk
275 g (9 oz) scallops or raw peeled
  prawns
1.25 kg (2½ lb) floury potatoes,
  thinly sliced
25 g (1 oz) butter
3 large shallots, finely chopped
4 tablespoons chopped tarragon
4 tablespoons chopped parsley
125 g (4 oz) Gruyère cheese,
  grated
Béchamel Sauce (see page 223)
salt and pepper

Serves **6**
Prep time **30 minutes**
Cooking time **1 hour**

1 Put the cod in a frying pan with the milk and seasoning. Cover and cook gently for 5 minutes. Add the scallops or prawns and cook, covered, for a further 2 minutes. Drain, reserving the liquid, and leave to cool.

2 Bring a saucepan of lightly salted water to the boil, add the potatoes, return to the boil and cook for 6-8 minutes or until just tender. Drain. Melt the butter in the rinsed-out frying pan and fry the shallots for 5 minutes. Stir in the herbs.

3 Flake the fish into large chunks, discarding any bones, and arrange in a large, shallow, ovenproof dish. Add the scallops or prawns, shallots and herbs.

4 Stir two-thirds of the cheese into the béchamel sauce along with the poaching juices. Pour half over the fish. Layer the potatoes over the top and pour over the remaining sauce. Scatter with the rest of the cheese and bake in a preheated oven, 190°C (375°F), Gas Mark 5, for about 40 minutes or until golden.

# SEAFOOD
# PAELLA

2 tablespoons olive oil
1 large onion, finely diced
1 garlic clove, crushed
1 red pepper, cored, deseeded and
  chopped into 5 mm (¼ inch) dice
300 g (10 oz) paella rice
1.5 litres (1¾ pints) hot Fish Stock
  (see page 235) or water
pinch of saffron threads
2 large tomatoes, roughly
  chopped
300 g (10 oz) raw peeled king
  prawns
200 g (7 oz) clams, cleaned
200 g (7 oz) mussels, scrubbed
  and debearded
200 g (7 oz) squid, cleaned and
  cut into rings, tentacles
  discarded
150 g (5 oz) frozen peas, thawed
2 tablespoons chopped parsley
salt and pepper

Serves **4**
Prep time **30 minutes**
Cooking time **25 minutes**

1 Heat the oil in a large frying pan, add the onion, garlic and red pepper and fry for a few minutes until they have started to soften. Add the rice, stir to coat and fry for 1 minute.

2 Pour enough stock over the rice to cover it by about 1 cm (½ inch). Add the saffron threads and stir well. Bring the mixture to the boil, add the tomatoes and reduce the heat to a simmer. Stir well once again, then simmer for 10-12 minutes, stirring occasionally so that the rice does not catch on the bottom of the pan.

3 Add the prawns, clams and mussels (discard any that do not shut when tapped) and squid to the pan, along with a little more water or stock if the rice is too dry. Cook until the clams and mussels open (discard any that do not open), the prawns are pink and the squid turns white and loses its transparency.

4 Stir in the peas and parsley and cook for a few more minutes until the peas are hot. Season to taste with salt and pepper and serve.

AFFORDABILITY 3

# **PAD** THAI

1 Cook the noodles in boiling water for 5 minutes until softened. Drain and immediately refresh under cold water. Drain again and set aside.

2 In a small bowl mix the soy sauce, lime juice and fish sauce with 1 tablespoon water and set aside.

3 Heat the oil in a wok or large frying pan, add the garlic and chilli and stir-fry over a medium heat for 30 seconds. Add the noodles and tofu and stir-fry for 2–3 minutes or until heated through.

4 Carefully push the noodle mixture up the side of the pan, clearing the centre of the pan. Add the eggs and heat gently for 1 minute without stirring, then gently start 'scrambling' the eggs with a spoon. Mix the noodles back into the centre and stir well until mixed with the eggs.

5 Add the soy sauce mixture and cook for 1 minute or until heated through. Stir in the bean sprouts and coriander. Spoon into bowls, scatter over the peanuts and serve immediately.

250 g (8 oz) dried rice noodles
1½ tablespoons sweet soy sauce
1½ tablespoons lime juice
1 tablespoons Thai fish sauce
   (nam pla)
3 tablespoons groundnut oil
2 garlic cloves, sliced
1 small red chilli, deseeded and
   chopped
125 g (4 oz) firm tofu, diced
2 eggs, lightly beaten
125 g (4 oz) bean sprouts
1 tablespoon chopped fresh
   coriander
4 tablespoons salted peanuts,
   chopped

Serves **2**
Prep time **10 minutes**
Cooking time **12 minutes**

# CHILLI PRAWNS WITH
# GARLIC & SPINACH

2 tablespoons vegetable oil
1 garlic clove, sliced
1 red bird's eye chilli, deseeded
  and chopped
300 g (10 oz) baby spinach
125 g (4 oz) raw peeled tiger
  prawns
3 tablespoons light soy sauce
2 teaspoons caster sugar
1 tablespoon Chinese rice wine or
  dry sherry
1 tablespoon Thai fish sauce
  (nam pla)
Chinese chive flowers or chives,
  to garnish

Serves **4**
Prep time **10 minutes**
Cooking time **5 minutes**

**1** Heat the oil in a wok over a high heat until the oil starts to shimmer, add the garlic and chilli and stir-fry for 30 seconds.

**2** Add the spinach and prawns and stir-fry in the oil for 1-2 minutes until the spinach begins to wilt and the prawns are pink and cooked through.

**3** Mix together the soy sauce, sugar, rice wine and fish sauce with 6 tablespoons water and add to the pan. Quickly stir-fry together for another minute, garnish with Chinese chive flowers or chives and serve while the spinach still has texture.

# SALMON FISHCAKES *WITH* **SPINACH** & POACHED EGGS

AFFORDABILITY 2

1 Put the potatoes in a saucepan of lightly salted boiling water and cook until they can just be pierced by a sharp knife. Drain well and leave to cool.

2 Roughly chop the salmon or process it briefly in a food processor to make a coarse mince. Use a fork or the back of a wooden spoon to mash the potatoes with salt and pepper. Add the minced salmon and mix together.

3 Flour your hands and divide the mixture into four equal pieces and press them firmly into plump fishcakes. Coat each cake in flour and chill in the refrigerator for 1 hour.

4 Heat the oil in a large frying pan, add the fishcakes and cook for 3-4 minutes on each side.

5 Meanwhile, put the spinach in a saucepan with just the water that clings to the leaves and cover with a lid. Heat gently for 2-3 minutes or until the spinach has just begun to wilt. Drain thoroughly and season with a little salt and pepper.

6 Poach the eggs in a pan of gently simmering water for 3-4 minutes until just cooked. Remove the fishcakes from the pan and set them on individual plates. Top each one with some of the spinach and finish with a hot poached egg. Serve with lemon wedges.

250 g (8 oz) King Edward
  potatoes, quartered
300 g (10 oz) salmon fillet, skinned
  and bones removed
1-2 tablespoons plain flour
6-8 tablespoons sunflower or
  groundnut oil
500 g (1 lb) spinach, washed
1 tablespoon vinegar
4 eggs
sea salt and pepper
lemon wedges, to serve

Serves **4**
Prep time **20 minutes, plus chilling**
Cooking time **25 minutes**

# GRILLED HADDOCK
# WITH LENTILS & SPINACH

2 teaspoons olive oil
1 onion, finely chopped
pinch of ground cumin
pinch of ground turmeric
pinch of dried red chilli flakes
250 g (8 oz) can lentils, rinsed and
   drained
175 g (6 oz) baby spinach leaves
4 tablespoons crème fraîche
2 skinless haddock fillet, about
   125 g (4 oz) each
lemon wedges, to garnish
grilled tomatoes, to serve

Serves **2**
Prep time **10 minutes**
Cooking time **15 minutes**

**1** Heat half the oil in a nonstick frying pan, add the onion and cook for about 5 minutes until softened. Add the cumin, turmeric and chilli flakes and cook, stirring, for 1 minute. Add the lentils, spinach and crème fraîche and cook gently for 4-5 minutes until the spinach has wilted.

**2** Meanwhile, brush both sides of the haddock with the remaining oil, put on a nonstick baking sheet and cook under a preheated high grill for 2-3 minutes on each side until just cooked through.

**3** Arrange the lentils and spinach mixture on warm serving plates and top with the haddock. Garnish with lemon wedges and serve with grilled tomatoes.

# CREAMY FISH
## *Lasagne*

CHUNKY, SUCCULENT PIECES OF FISH ARE A MUST FOR THIS DISH SO THEY'RE NOT COMPLETELY LOST BETWEEN THE LAYERS OF PASTA AND SAUCE. IF YOU USE DRIED LASAGNE SHEETS COOK THEM FIRST UNTIL THEY ARE JUST TENDER.

1 Put the tomatoes, onion, garlic, tomato paste and a little seasoning in a large saucepan and bring to the boil. Cook for about 10 minutes or until the mixture is thick and pulpy. Stir in half the anchovies and lay the haddock on top. Cook gently for 5 minutes or until the fish is opaque.

2 Spoon one-third of the mixture into a shallow, 1.2 litre (2 pint) ovenproof dish, making sure the pieces of fish are evenly distributed. Arrange a layer of lasagne sheets on top. Cover with half the remaining tomato and fish mixture and spoon over one-third of the cheese sauce. Place another layer of lasagne on top and cover with the remaining tomatoes and fish. Add the remaining lasagne and spoon over the rest of the sauce.

3 Tear the bread into pieces and blend in a food processor to make coarse breadcrumbs. Add the remaining anchovies and blend again until mixed.

4 Scatter the breadcrumbs over the lasagne and drizzle with the oil. Bake in a preheated oven, 180°C (350°F), Gas Mark 4, for about 45 minutes or until golden. Leave to stand for 10 minutes before serving.

2 x 400 g (13 oz) cans chopped tomatoes
1 large onion, finely chopped
2 garlic cloves, crushed
3 tablespoons sun-dried tomato paste
50 g (2 oz) can anchovy fillets in olive oil, drained and chopped
700 g (1 lb 7 oz) skinned haddock fillet, cut into chunks
125 g (4 oz) fresh lasagne sheets
Rich Cheese Sauce (see page 224)
40 g (1½ oz) bread
2 tablespoons olive oil
salt and pepper

Serves **4-5**
Prep time **25 minutes, plus standing**
Cooking time **1 hour**

# CHERRY TOMATO & RICOTTA PENNE

300 g (10 oz) dried penne
3 tablespoons olive oil
1 onion, chopped
4 garlic cloves, crushed
1 tablespoon chopped oregano
325 g (11 oz) cherry tomatoes,
   halved
1 teaspoon caster sugar
3 tablespoons sun-dried tomato
   paste
250 g (8 oz) ricotta cheese
salt and pepper

Serves **4**
Prep time **5 minutes**
Cooking time **10 minutes**

**1** Cook the pasta in a large saucepan of lightly salted boiling water for about 10 minutes or until just tender.

**2** Meanwhile, heat the oil in a frying pan, add the onion and fry gently for 3 minutes. Add the garlic, oregano, tomatoes and sugar and fry quickly, stirring, for 1 minute. Add the tomato paste and 6 tablespoons of water, season to taste with salt and pepper and bring to the boil. Add dessertspoonfuls of the ricotta cheese to the pan and heat through gently for 1 minute.

**3** Drain the pasta and pile on to serving plates. Spoon the tomato and cheese mixture on top, taking care not to break up the ricotta too much. Serve immediately.

AFFORDABILITY
**1**

### Buy in bulk

Look out for bulk-buy specials on dry goods such as pasta, rice, cereal, jars and tins. They will usually last for a few months, and you could save yourself a fortune on food that you know you're going to use – as long as you've got room under your bed for ten trays of baked beans.

# RIBBON PASTA WITH AUBERGINES *&* PINE NUTS

1 Heat the oil in a large frying pan or sauté pan and fry the aubergines and onions for 8-10 minutes until golden and tender. Add the pine nuts and garlic and fry for 2 minutes. Stir in the tomato paste and stock and cook for 2 minutes.

2 Meanwhile, cook the pasta in a large saucepan of lightly salted boiling water for 2 minutes or until just tender.

3 Drain the pasta and return to the pan. Add the sauce and olives, season to taste with salt and pepper and toss together over a moderate heat for 1 minute until combined. Scatter over the parsley and serve immediately.

8 tablespoons olive oil
2 aubergines, diced
2 red onions, sliced
75 g (3 oz) pine nuts
3 garlic cloves, crushed
5 tablespoons sun-dried tomato paste
150 ml (¼ pint) Vegetable Stock (see page 235)
300 g (10 oz) fresh ribbon pasta
100 g (3½ oz) pitted black olives
salt and pepper
3 tablespoons roughly chopped flat leaf parsley, to garnish

Serves **4**
Prep time **5 minutes**
Cooking time **17-20 minutes**

# CHERRY TOMATO **TARTS** WITH **PESTO CRÈME FRAÎCHE**

2 tablespoons extra virgin olive oil
1 onion, finely chopped
375 g (12 oz) cherry tomatoes
2 garlic cloves, crushed
3 tablespoons sun-dried tomato
  paste
325 g (11 oz) ready-rolled puff
  pastry (thawed if frozen)
beaten egg, to glaze
150 ml (¼ pint) crème fraîche
2 tablespoons Pesto
  (see page 228)
salt and pepper
basil leaves, to garnish

Serves **4**
Prep time **10 minutes**
Cooking time **18 minutes**

**1** Lightly grease a large baking sheet and sprinkle with water. Heat the oil in a frying pan, add the onion and fry for about 3 minutes until softened. Halve about 150 g (5 oz) of the tomatoes. Remove the pan from the heat, add the garlic and tomato paste, then stir in all the tomatoes, turning until they are lightly coated in the sauce.

**2** Unroll the pastry on a lightly floured surface and cut out four 12 cm (5 inch) rounds, using a cutter or small bowl as a guide. Transfer to the baking sheet and use the tip of a sharp knife to make a shallow cut 1 cm (½ inch) from the edge of each round to form a rim. (Do not cut all the way through the pastry.) Brush the rims with beaten egg. Pile the tomato mixture on the centres of the pastry circles making sure the mixture stays within the rims. Bake the tarts in a preheated oven, 220°C (425°F), Gas Mark 7, for about 15 minutes until the pastry is risen and golden.

**3** Meanwhile, lightly mix together the crème fraîche, pesto and salt and pepper in a bowl so that the crème fraîche is streaked with the pesto.

**4** Transfer the cooked tarts to serving plates and spoon over the crème fraîche and pesto mixture. Serve scattered with basil leaves.

# MUSHROOM & BROCCOLI PIE

1 Cook the broccoli in a large saucepan of lightly salted boiling water for about 2 minutes or until the florets are just beginning to soften.

2 Meanwhile, heat the oil in a large frying pan and cook the mushrooms over a medium heat, stirring occasionally, for about 5 minutes. Stir in the Gorgonzola, mascarpone and crème fraîche. Add the drained broccoli florets and the chives and season to taste with salt and pepper. Spoon the mixture into four individual ovenproof dishes or a single large rectangular ovenproof dish.

3 Lay the pastry over the filling, pressing it to the sides of the dish to seal. Brush the top with beaten egg and cut two slits in the pastry to allow steam to escape. Cook in a preheated oven, 220°C (425°F), Gas Mark 7, for about 25 minutes until the pastry is crisp and golden. Serve immediately.

350 g (11½ oz) broccoli florets
3 tablespoons olive oil
350 g (11½ oz) mushrooms, trimmed and thickly sliced
150 g (5 oz) Gorgonzola cheese
3 tablespoons mascarpone cheese
4 tablespoons crème fraîche
2 tablespoons chopped chives
1 large sheet ready-rolled puff pastry (thawed if frozen)
1 egg, lightly beaten
salt and pepper

Serves **4**
Prep time **8 minutes**
Cooking time **30 minutes**

# VEGETABLE BOLOGNESE

½ tablespoon vegetable oil
1 onion, chopped
200 g (7 oz) can baby carrots, drained and chopped
1 leek, sliced
2 celery sticks, sliced
400 g (13 oz) can chopped tomatoes
1 tablespoon tomato purée
1 teaspoon cayenne pepper
125 g (4 oz) mushrooms, sliced
375 g (12 oz) spaghetti
salt and pepper
basil leaves, to garnish

1 Heat the oil in a saucepan, add the onion and fry over a low heat for 3-5 minutes or until soft. Stir in the carrots, leek and celery. Add the tomatoes, tomato purée, cayenne pepper and mushrooms and stir to combine. Season to taste with salt and pepper and simmer for 10 minutes.

2 Meanwhile, cook the spaghetti in a large saucepan of lightly salted boiling water for 8-10 minutes or according to the pack instructions until just tender. Drain the pasta and sprinkle with pepper.

3 Mound the spaghetti on serving plates, spoon the sauce over the top and serve garnished with a few basil leaves.

Serves **4**
Prep time **10 minutes**
Cooking time **15 minutes**

AFFORDABILITY
1

## Pep up pasta sauces

Spruce up cheap jars of pasta sauce with a handful of olives, a sprinkle of dried chilli flakes or a few chopped herbs. Tins of chopped tomatoes also tend to be fairly cheap, so you can add the same to these and enjoy a budget meal with a bit of pizzazz for just a few more pence.

# SPINACH, ONION & CREAM CHEESE PIZZA

**1** Lightly grease a large baking sheet. Put the flour in a bowl with the oil and salt. Add 100 ml (3½ fl oz water) and mix to a soft dough, adding a little more water, a teaspoonful at a time, if the dough is too dry. Roll out on a floured surface into a circle about 28 cm (11 inches) across. Put the dough circle on the baking sheet and bake in a preheated oven, 230°C (450°F), Gas Mark 8, for 5 minutes until a crust has formed.

**2** Make the topping. Beat together the cream cheese, crème fraîche, rosemary and a little salt and pepper.

**3** Heat the oil in a frying pan and fry the onion for 3-4 minutes or until softened. Add the spinach and a little salt and pepper and cook, stirring, for about 1 minute until the spinach has just wilted.

**4** Pile the spinach on to the pizza base, spreading it to within 1 cm (½ inch) of the edge. Place spoonfuls of the cheese mixture over the spinach. Bake for a further 8 minutes or until turning golden.

3 tablespoons olive oil, plus extra for greasing
250 g (8 oz) self-raising flour
1 teaspoon salt

**Topping**
100 g (3½ oz) full-fat soft cheese
100 ml (3½ fl oz) crème fraîche
2 teaspoons chopped rosemary
3 tablespoons olive oil
1 large onion, finely sliced
375 g (12 oz) young spinach
salt and pepper

Serves **4**
Prep time **25 minutes**
Cooking time **15 minutes**

# **PIZZA** FIORENTINA

1 tablespoon olive oil, plus extra
   for drizzling and glazing
2 garlic cloves, crushed
500 g (1 lb) baby spinach
plain flour, for dusting
4 ready-made pizza bases, about
   23 cm (9 inches) across
200 ml (7 fl oz) passata
200 g (7 oz) mozzarella cheese,
   drained and chopped
20 black olives
4 eggs
salt and pepper

Serves **4**
Prep time **20 minutes**
Cooking time **40 minutes**

**1** Heat the oil in a large frying pan with the garlic for 15 seconds. Add the spinach and cook over a high heat for 1-2 minutes until just wilted. Season lightly with salt and pepper.

**2** Put a baking sheet in a preheated oven, 240°C (475°F), Gas Mark 9. Put a pizza base in a well-floured, 23 cm (9 inch) loose-bottomed tart tin.

**3** Spoon 3 tablespoons passata over the base and scatter over a quarter of the mozzarella, spinach and olives. Crack 1 egg on to the pizza, drizzle with oil and season lightly with salt and pepper. Brush the border with oil to glaze, if liked. Remove the baking sheet from the oven, slide the tin on to it and quickly return to the oven. Bake for 7-8 minutes until cooked and bubbling. Serve immediately. As the first pizza cooks, prepare the next for the oven.

AFFORDABILITY
**1**

# PIZZA PUFF PIES

AFFORDABILITY

1

1 Heat the oil in saucepan, add the onion and fry for 5 minutes until softened. Add the garlic, tomatoes and sugar and season to taste with salt and pepper. Cover and simmer gently for 15 minutes, stirring from time to time until the sauce has thickened. Leave to cool slightly.

2 Cut the pastry into six pieces. Roll out each piece on a lightly floured surface and trim to a 15 cm (6 inch) circle using a saucer or cutter as a guide. Press each pastry circle into the base of a lightly oiled metal Yorkshire pudding tin or tart tin, 10 cm (4 inches) across and 2.5 cm (1 inch) deep, and press the pastry at intervals to the sides of the tin to give a wavy edge.

3 Keeping about half the smaller basil leaves for garnish, tear the larger leaves into pieces and stir into the sauce. Divide the sauce between the pies and spread to give an even layer. Cut the mozzarella into 6 slices and add a slice to each pizza. Sprinkle the mozzarella with a little salt and pepper and add an olive to each, if used.

4 Bake in a preheated oven, 200°C (400°F), Gas Mark 6, for 20 minutes until the pastry is crisp and golden. Leave to cool for 5 minutes, then turn out. Drizzle with a little olive oil, if liked, and sprinkle with the remaining basil leaves. Serve warm with salad.

1 tablespoon olive oil
1 onion, chopped
1 garlic clove, finely chopped
400 g (13 oz) can chopped tomatoes
1 teaspoon caster sugar
500 g (1 lb) puff pastry (thawed if frozen)
small bunch of basil
125 g (4 oz) mozzarella cheese, drained
6 pitted black olives (optional)
salt and pepper

**To serve**
olive oil (optional)
green salad

Makes **6**
Prep time **25 minutes**
Cooking time **40 minutes**

# GRILLED COURGETTES
## *with* GOATS' CHEESE

5 large courgettes, diagonally
sliced
2 tablespoons extra virgin olive oil
1-2 garlic cloves, finely diced
100 g (3½ oz) soft goats' cheese
30 g (1 oz) pine nuts, toasted
salt and pepper

Serves **4**
Prep time **10 minutes**
Cooking time **5 minutes**

**1** Brush the courgette slices with 1 tablespoon oil and cook
in a hot griddle pan for 1-2 minutes each side. The
courgettes should be cooked but still firm. Season to taste
with salt and pepper.

**2** Heat the remaining oil in a small frying pan over a medium
heat and gently fry the garlic for 1 minute.

**3** Transfer the courgettes to a warm serving plate and
crumble over the goats' cheese. Scatter over the pine nuts
and drizzle the garlic oil on top. Serve immediately.

AFFORDABILITY

2

# PESTO ALLA GENOVESE

IN GENOA, THE HOME OF PESTO, THIS AROMATIC PASTA IS TRADITIONALLY COOKED WITH POTATOES AND GREEN BEANS. THIS MIGHT SOUND UNUSUAL, BUT IT IS TRULY A HEAVENLY COMBINATION.

75 g (3 oz) basil leaves
25 g (1 oz) pine nuts
2 garlic cloves, crushed
2 tablespoons grated Parmesan cheese, plus extra to serve
1 tablespoon grated pecorino cheese
3 tablespoons olive oil
250 g (8 oz) potatoes, peeled and thinly sliced
400 g (13 oz) dried trenette or linguine
150 g (5 oz) green beans

Serves **4**
Prep time **30 minutes**
Cooking time **20 minutes**

1 Use a pestle and mortar to grind together the basil, pine nuts and garlic to form a paste. Stir in the cheeses, then slowly add the oil, a little at a time, stirring all the time with a wooden spoon. Alternatively, blend the basil, pine nuts and garlic in a food processor until the mixture forms a paste. Add the cheeses and process briefly. Then, with the motor still running, pour in the oil through the feed tube in a thin, steady stream.

2 Cook the potatoes in a large saucepan of lightly salted boiling water for 5 minutes, then add the pasta and cook according to the pack instructions or until just tender. Add the beans 5 minutes before the end of the cooking time.

3 Drain the pasta and vegetables, reserving 2 tablespoons of the cooking water. Return the cooked pasta and vegetables to the pan and stir in the pesto sauce, adding as much of the reserved water as needed to loosen the mixture. Serve immediately, scattered with some extra grated Parmesan.

# ROAST POTATOES WITH ROSEMARY & GARLIC

**AFFORDABILITY 1**

1 Cut the potatoes lengthways into quarters and pat them dry on kitchen paper.

2 Put half the oil in a large roasting tin and place in a preheated oven, 230°C (450°F), Gas Mark 8..

3 Mix together the remaining oil and the rosemary and toss the potatoes in the oil to coat them completely. Add the potatoes to the roasting tin in the oven, shake carefully so they are in an even layer, then place the tin at the top of the oven and cook for 20 minutes.

4 Remove the tin from the oven and turn the potatoes so that they cook evenly. Scatter the garlic among the potatoes, return the tin to the oven and cook for a further 5 minutes. Remove the potatoes from the oven, season with salt and pepper and serve immediately.

750 g (1½ lb) potatoes, unpeeled
4 tablespoons olive oil
2 tablespoons chopped rosemary
4 garlic cloves, thinly sliced
salt and pepper

Serves **4**
Prep time **5 minutes**
Cooking time **25 minutes**

# PATATAS *Bravas*

THIS VERSION OF THE CLASSIC SPANISH DISH USES A THICK, RICH TOMATO SAUCE, WHILE THE POTATOES RETAIN THEIR CRISP, APPETIZING TEXTURE.

5 tablespoons olive oil
800 g (1 lb 10 oz) potatoes, cubed
1 red onion, chopped
2 bay leaves
½ teaspoon hot paprika
2 garlic cloves, crushed
4 tomatoes, skinned and chopped
2 tablespoons sun-dried tomato paste
salt
3 tablespoons flat leaf parsley, roughly chopped, to garnish

Serves **6**
Prep time **20 minutes**
Cooking time **25 minutes**

**1** Heat 3 tablespoons oil in a large frying pan, add the potatoes and a pinch of salt and fry gently, stirring frequently, for 15 minutes until golden.

**2** Meanwhile, in a separate pan heat the remaining oil and fry the onion with the bay leaves for 5 minutes. Add the paprika and garlic and fry for a further minute.

**3** Stir in the tomatoes, tomato paste, half the parsley and 2 tablespoons water. Cover and cook for 8–10 minutes, stirring occasionally to break up the tomatoes.

**4** Add the tomato sauce to the potatoes and cook for a further 5 minutes, adding a dash of water if the sauce loses its juiciness. Check the seasoning, garnish with parsley and serve hot.

AFFORDABILITY
1

# GRILLED VEGETABLE & HALOUMI SALAD

**1** Put the tomatoes and mushrooms in a roasting tin, drizzle with about 2 tablespoons oil, season to taste with salt and pepper and cook in a preheated oven, 180°C (350°F), Gas Mark 4, for 10 minutes.

**2** Meanwhile, cut the courgettes into batons about 4 x 2 cm (1½ x ¾ inches) and put them in a large bowl with the trimmed asparagus. Drizzle with olive oil and a pinch of salt and pepper.

**3** Heat a griddle pan over a high heat and grill the asparagus and courgettes. Transfer the asparagus and courgettes to the oven with the other vegetables and cook for a further 6-8 minutes.

**4** Cut the haloumi into 5 mm (¼ inch) slices. Heat 1 teaspoon olive oil in a large frying pan over a medium heat and cook the cheese slices until golden.

**5** Make the dressing by whisking the oil and vinegar. Stack the vegetables on serving plates, top with slices of cheese, spoon over the dressing and serve.

12 cherry tomatoes on the vine
4 portobello mushrooms
2-3 tablespoons olive oil
2 courgettes
500 g (1 lb) asparagus
250 g (8 oz) haloumi cheese
salt and pepper

**Dressing**
2 tablespoons olive oil
2 tablespoons balsamic vinegar

Serves **4**
Prep time **15 minutes**
Cooking time **25 minutes**

AFFORDABILITY
1

AFFORDABILITY 1

# MINT & LEMON GRASS TEA

THIS CALMING TEA STIMULATES THE DIGESTION, SO IT'S PERFECT FOR SERVING TO GUESTS AFTER A LARGE MEAL.

4 lemon grass stalks, lightly
   crushed to release the oils
small handful of mint leaves
1 tablespoon honey (optional)

Serves **4**
Prep time **5 minutes, plus**
**infusing**
Cooking time **5-6 minutes**

1 Bring 750 ml (1¼ pints) water to the boil in a large saucepan. Add the lemon grass stalks and boil for 5-6 minutes. Remove from the heat.

2 Add the mint leaves and honey, if used, cover and allow to infuse for 10 minutes.

3 Serve in cups or glasses. If you prefer, serve the mixture chilled, in a tall glass with plenty of ice.

# GREEN TEA

1 Put ¾-1 teaspoon green tea leaves (to taste, whether strong or weak) in a cup. Boil the water, but wait 3 minutes before pouring it over the leaves.

2 Add the water and leave to infuse for 1-5 minutes. To add more fragrance, put a few fresh mint leaves or any other herb or spice (such as saffron, mint, orange tree blossoms or cloves) into the cup. The tea is best drunk without sugar.

¾-1 teaspoon green tea leaves
small handful of fresh herbs or spices (optional)

Serves **1**
Prep time **2 minutes, plus infusing**

AFFORDABILITY
1

SWEETCORN & PEPPER FRITTATA

CHICKEN WITH SWEET
POTATO WEDGES

EGG-FRIED RICE

CAULIFLOWER CHEESE

# STRAPPED FOR CASH

# SOUTHERN FRIED CHICKEN

AFFORDABILITY 2

500 g (1 lb) sweet potatoes, peeled
500 g (1 lb) baking potatoes, scrubbed
6 tablespoons sunflower oil
1½ teaspoons smoked paprika
1½ teaspoons dried oregano
1 teaspoon dried mustard powder
1 teaspoon dried crushed red chillies
4 tablespoons plain flour
2 eggs, beaten
125 g (4 oz) fresh breadcrumbs
4 chicken thigh and drumstick joints
salt and pepper

**To serve**
mayonnaise
green salad

Serves **4**
Prep time **25 minutes**
Cooking time **35-40 minutes**

1 Thickly slice the sweet and baking potatoes and cut them into thick wedges. Mix 3 tablespoons oil with 1 teaspoon paprika, 1 teaspoon oregano, ½ teaspoon mustard, ½ teaspoon chilli seeds and some salt in a large plastic bag or bowl. Add the potatoes and toss in the mixture to coat.

2 Mix the remaining paprika, oregano, mustard and chilli seeds with the flour on a large plate and season to taste. Mix the eggs with 2 tablespoons water in a shallow dish and put the breadcrumbs on a second large plate.

3 Coat the chicken pieces in the flour mixture, then the beaten egg and then the breadcrumbs until completely covered.

4 Heat a large roasting tin in a preheated oven, 200°C (400°F), Gas Mark 6, for 5 minutes. Meanwhile, heat the remaining oil in a large frying pan, add the chicken and fry until pale golden. Transfer the chicken to the hot roasting tin, add the potatoes and roast for 30-35 minutes until the chicken is cooked through and the potatoes are crisp and golden. Transfer to serving plates and serve with mayonnaise and salad.

# CHICKEN WITH
## PEANUT SAUCE

**1** Heat a griddle pan or ordinary nonstick frying pan, add the chicken breasts and cook for 8-10 minutes on each side.

**2** Meanwhile, put the soy sauce, peanut butter, lemon juice and a little pepper in a small saucepan. Mix with 4 tablespoons water and heat gently, adjusting the consistency of the sauce with a little more water if necessary so that it is slightly runny but coats the back of a spoon.

**3** When the chicken is cooked, serve with the peanut sauce drizzled over the top, garnished with coriander and chopped fried peanuts, if liked. Serve with mixed vegetable noodles.

4 x 125 g (4 oz) boneless, skinless chicken breasts
1 tablespoon soy sauce
2 tablespoons crunchy or smooth peanut butter
4 tablespoons lemon juice
4 tablespoons water
pepper

**To garnish**
coriander leaves
peanuts, fried, chopped (optional)

Serves **4**
Prep time **5 minutes**
Cooking time **16-20 minutes**

AFFORDABILITY 2

# *FAST* CHICKEN **CURRY**

3 tablespoons olive oil
1 onion, finely chopped
4 tablespoons medium curry paste
8 boneless, skinless chicken
  thighs, cut into thin strips
400 g (13 oz) can chopped
  tomatoes
250 g (8 oz) broccoli, broken into
  small florets, and stalks peeled
  and sliced
100 ml (3½ fl oz) coconut milk
salt and pepper

1 Heat the oil in a deep, nonstick saucepan, add the onion and cook for 3 minutes until soft. Add the curry paste and cook, stirring, for 1 minute.

2 Add the chicken, tomatoes, broccoli and coconut milk to the pan. Bring to the boil, reduce the heat, cover and cook over a low heat for 15-20 minutes.

3 Remove from the heat, season well with salt and pepper and serve immediately.

Serves **4**
Prep time **5 minutes**
Cooking time **20-25 minutes**

# JERK
## CHICKEN WINGS

1 Put the chicken wings in a non-metallic dish. In a small bowl whisk together the oil, jerk seasoning mix, lemon juice and salt. Pour the mixture over the chicken and stir well until evenly coated. Cover and leave to marinate in the refrigerator for at least 30 minutes or overnight.

2 Arrange the chicken wings on a grill rack and cook under a preheated grill, basting halfway through cooking with any remaining marinade, for 6 minutes on each side or until cooked through, tender and lightly charred at the edges. Increase or reduce the temperature setting of the grill if necessary to make sure that the wings cook through. Garnish with chopped parsley and serve immediately with lemon wedges for squeezing over.

12 large chicken wings
2 tablespoons olive oil
1 tablespoon jerk seasoning mix
2 tablespoons lemon juice
1 teaspoon salt
chopped flat leaf parsley, to garnish
lemon wedges, to serve

Serves **4**
Prep time **5 minutes, plus marinating**
Cooking time **12 minutes**

# CHICKEN WITH
## SWEET POTATO
# WEDGES

4 sweet potatoes, about 1.25 kg
(2½ lb) in total, scrubbed
4 boneless, skinless chicken
thighs, cut into chunks
1 red onion, cut into wedges
4 plum tomatoes, cut into chunks
150 g (5 oz) chorizo in one piece,
skinned, sliced or diced
depending on diameter
3 stems rosemary, leaves torn
from stems
4 tablespoons olive oil
salt and pepper
watercress salad, to serve
(optional)

Serves **4**
Prep time **20 minutes**
Cooking time **35 minutes**

1 Cut the potatoes in half and then into thick wedges. Put them into a large roasting tin with the chicken, onion and tomatoes. Tuck the chorizo in and around the potatoes, then sprinkle with the rosemary and some salt and pepper.

2 Drizzle over the oil and cook in a preheated oven, 200°C (400°F), Gas Mark 6, for about 35 minutes, turning once or twice until the chicken is golden and cooked through and the potato wedges are browned and tender.

3 Spoon on to serving plates and serve as it is, or with a watercress salad.

# STEAK MEATLOAF

SERVE THIS MEATLOAF HOT OR COLD, DEPENDING ON THE WEATHER AND
CIRCUMSTANCES. LEFTOVERS, ACCOMPANIED WITH SALAD AND CHUTNEY,
MAKE AN IDEAL LUNCHTIME SNACK.

**1** Put the peppers and onion in a roasting tin, shake gently so they are in an even layer, drizzle with the oil and cook in a preheated oven, 200°C (400°F), Gas Mark 6, for 30 minutes until lightly roasted. Chop roughly when they are cooked. Reduce the heat to 160°C (325°F), Gas Mark 3.

**2** Use some bacon to line the base and long sides of a 1 kg (2 lb) loaf tin, overlapping them slightly and letting the ends overhang the sides. Finely chop the rest.

**3** Mix together the steak and pork minces, chopped bacon, roasted vegetables, herbs, Worcestershire sauce, tomato paste, breadcrumbs, egg and seasoning. Pack the mixture into the tin and fold the ends of the bacon over the filling. Cover with kitchen foil, place in a roasting tin and pour in boiling water to a depth of 1.5 cm (¾ inch). Cook in the oven for 2 hours.

**4** To serve hot leave for 15 minutes, then invert on to a serving plate. To serve cold leave to cool in the tin, then remove and wrap in foil.

2 red peppers, cored, deseeded
  and cut into chunks
1 red onion, sliced
3 tablespoons olive oil
300 g (10 oz) thin-cut streaky
  bacon
500 g (1 lb) lean steak mince
250 g (8 oz) pork mince
2 tablespoons chopped oregano
2 tablespoons chopped parsley
3 tablespoons Worcestershire
  sauce
2 tablespoons sun-dried tomato
  paste
50 g (2 oz) fresh breadcrumbs
1 egg
salt and pepper

Serves **6**
Prep time **30 minutes**
Cooking time **2½ hours**

AFFORDABILITY
2

2 tablespoons oil
500 g (1 lb) lean minced lamb
1 onion, finely chopped
2 carrots, finely chopped
2 celery sticks, finely chopped
1 garlic clove, finely chopped
1 tablespoon plain flour
300 ml (½ pint) Chicken or
  Lamb Stock (see page 234)
2 tablespoons tomato paste
400 g (13 oz) can baked beans
1 kg (2 lb) floury potatoes
50 g (2 oz) butter
3-4 tablespoons milk
25 g (1 oz) grated Cheddar
  cheese (optional)
salt and pepper

Serves **4**
Prep time **20 minutes**
Cooking time **1 hour 20
minutes-1½ hours**

AFFORDABILITY
**1**

# SHEPHERD'S PIE

**1** Heat the oil in a large, heavy-based saucepan and fry the lamb, stirring, until lightly browned. Add the vegetables and garlic and fry for 5 minutes.

**2** Stir in the flour, stock and tomato paste, season to taste with salt and pepper and heat until bubbling. Cook gently for 30 minutes until the lamb is tender, adding a little water or more stock if the mixture starts to dry out. Stir in the beans and turn into a shallow ovenproof dish.

**3** Meanwhile, cook the potatoes in a large saucepan of lightly salted boiling water until tender. Drain and return to the pan. Mash well with the butter, milk and seasoning. Spoon the mash over the meat mixture, spreading it in an even layer with a fork. Cook in a preheated oven, 190°C (375°F), Gas Mark 5, for 30-40 minutes until pale golden.

**4** For a crispy crust pop the pie under the grill before serving, with or without a sprinkling of grated cheese.

# SAUSAGE
# MEATBALLS,
## PEAS & PASTA

1 Cut the sausages into small pieces and roll into walnut-sized balls.

2 Heat half the oil in a large, nonstick frying pan, add the meatballs and cook over a medium heat, stirring frequently, for 10 minutes until cooked through. Remove from the pan with a slotted spoon.

3 Meanwhile, plunge the pasta into a large saucepan of lightly salted boiling water. Return to the boil and cook for 8 minutes. Add the peas, return to the boil and cook for a further 2 minutes until the peas and pasta are just tender. Drain well, reserving 4 tablespoons of the cooking water.

4 Add the garlic, sage and chilli flakes to the meatball pan, season to taste with salt and pepper and cook over a low heat for 2-3 minutes until the garlic is soft but not browned. Return the meatballs to the pan and stir.

5 Return the pasta and peas to the saucepan and stir in the meatball mixture, reserved cooking water and remaining oil and heat through for 2 minutes. Serve in bowls topped with grated Parmesan.

500 g (1 lb) beef or pork sausages, skins removed
4 tablespoons extra virgin olive oil
400 g (13 oz) dried fusilli
250 g (8 oz) frozen peas (thawed)
2 garlic cloves, sliced
2 tablespoons chopped sage
½ teaspoon dried chilli flakes
salt and black pepper
grated Parmesan cheese, to serve

Serves **4**
Prep time **20 minutes**
Cooking time **15 minutes**

# BEEF GOULASH

4 tablespoons olive oil
1.5 kg (3 lb) braising steak, cubed
2 onions, sliced
2 red peppers, cored, deseeded
  and diced
1 tablespoon smoked paprika
2 tablespoons chopped marjoram
1 teaspoon caraway seeds
1 litre (1¾ pints) Beef Stock (see
  page 234)
5 tablespoons tomato purée
salt and pepper

Serves **8**
Prep time **10 minutes**
Cooking time **2-2½ hours**

**1** Heat the oil in a large, heavy-based saucepan, add the beef, in three batches, and cook over a high heat for 5 minutes until browned all over. Remove from the pan with a slotted spoon.

**2** Add the onions and red peppers to the pan and cook gently for 10 minutes until softened. Stir in the paprika, marjoram and caraway seeds and cook, stirring, for a further minute.

**3** Return the beef to the pan, add the stock, tomato purée and salt and pepper to taste and bring to the boil, stirring. Reduce the heat, cover and simmer gently for 1½-2 hours. Remove the lid for the final 30 minutes if the sauce needs thickening.

## Double up and freeze

If you're cooking a spaghetti Bolognese, chilli or curry, double up on the ingredients and freeze half. It won't take any longer to cook but you'll have a ready-prepared meal in the freezer for the next time you can't be bothered to cook, or can't afford a trip to the shops.

# MONEY
## MATTERS

Budget. It's a nasty word, but it's one you'll be hearing a lot during your time at uni. With student grants consigned to the annals of history and fees threatening to soak up your disposable income as soon as you land a job, you need to do everything you can to make your meagre funds stretch as far as possible.

## BILLS, BILLS, BILLS

This can often be a bone of contention in student households, with loose change being counted out every time a utility bill arrives. You can save yourselves a lot of hassle (and some money) by switching all your utility bills to direct debit so that you know exactly how much you're paying each month, and you won't get any nasty surprises after a bitterly cold winter in a energy-inefficient house. If there are just two or three of you it's worth getting a household bank account, with each of you paying in a monthly sum to cover all the household expenses.

If you're shopping independently make food ownership rights clear from the start – a piece of cake or coveted pint of milk could cause a major incident if one person doesn't respect the food rules. However, if you plan to shop as a household then it's a good idea to have someone who doesn't mind taking charge of collecting money and making a communal shopping list. You will probably be looking at somewhere in the region of £15–20 a week for each person on food, but obviously this will depend on where you live and what supermarkets, markets and so on are nearby. Clubbing together can work out a lot cheaper because you can buy bigger (so more economical) packets of cereal, margarine, cartons of milk and vegetables. Here are a few more tips to make your food budget stretch even further:

- Wait for closing time at the supermarket – that's when the prices drop.

- Look out for BOGOF deals (that's buy one, get one free, to you and me).

- Ditch take-aways in favour of supermarket equivalents, much cheaper.

- Make your own lunch – ok, it's not as cool as a latte and ciabatta at the canteen, but you'll save a fortune.

- If there's a sell-by date food bargain, buy it and freeze it for another time.

- Choose all the food you want online so you know exactly how much it will cost. Then go and buy it yourself and save on the delivery charge.

# CALF'S LIVER & BACON

FRY THE LIVER A LITTLE LONGER THAN SUGGESTED IN THE RECIPE IF YOU PREFER IT COOKED THROUGH, BUT TAKE CARE NOT TO COOK IT FOR TOO LONG OR IT WILL START TO TOUGHEN UP.

2 teaspoons plain flour
625 g (1½ lb) calf's liver
25 g (1 oz) butter
1 tablespoon olive oil
12 large sage leaves
8 rashers of back bacon
150 ml (½ pint) dry cider
salt and pepper

Serves **4**
Prep time **10 minutes**
Cooking time **6-8 minutes**

**1** Season the flour with salt and pepper. Cut away any tubes from the liver and dust it with the flour.

**2** Melt half the butter with the oil in a large frying pan until bubbling. Add the sage leaves and cook for about 30 seconds until sizzling. Drain and transfer to a plate with a slotted spoon.

**3** Fry the bacon until golden, drain and transfer to the plate and keep warm. Add the liver to the pan and fry for about 2 minutes until deep golden. Turn the slices and return the bacon and sage to the pan. Cook for a further 1-2 minutes. (At this stage the liver will be slightly pink in the centre but cook a little more if preferred.) Drain and keep warm.

**4** Add the cider to the pan and let it bubble until slightly reduced, scraping up any residue. Whisk in the remaining butter and check the seasoning. Transfer the liver and bacon to serving plates, spoon over the sauce and scatter with the sage leaves.

# EGG-FRIED
# RICE

1  Put the eggs, ginger and half the soy sauce in a bowl and whisk lightly to combine.

2  Heat the oil in a wok over a high heat until the oil starts to shimmer. Pour in the egg mixture and use a spatula to scramble it for 30-60 seconds, until just cooked.

3  Add the cold cooked rice, spring onions, sesame oil and remaining soy sauce and stir-fry for 1-2 minutes or until the rice is steaming hot.

4 eggs
2 teaspoons chopped fresh root ginger
1½ tablespoons light soy sauce
2 tablespoons groundnut oil
300 g (10 oz) cold cooked jasmine rice (200 g/7 oz raw weight)
2 spring onions, finely sliced
¼ teaspoon sesame oil

Serves **2**
Prep time **5 minutes**
Cooking time **4 minutes**

AFFORDABILITY
1

# CROQUE MONSIEUR

100 g (3½ oz) butter, softened
8 slices of white bread
4 slices of Cheddar cheese
4 slices of cooked ham
4 tablespoons vegetable oil
pepper

Serves **4**
Prep time **10 minutes**
Cooking time **10 minutes**

1 Spread half the butter over one side of each slice of bread. Put a slice of Cheddar on four of the buttered slices, top with a slice of ham and sprinkle with pepper. Top with the remaining slices of bread, butter side down, and press down hard.

2 Melt half the rest of the butter with half the oil in a large frying pan, and fry two sandwiches until golden brown, turning once. Cook the remaining sandwiches in the same way, cut into halves and serve immediately.

AFFORDABILITY
1

# BLT
## Sandwich

1 Heat a small, nonstick frying pan and cook the bacon, turning once, until it is golden brown and crisp. Remove and drain on kitchen paper.

2 Toast the bread on both sides. Spread one side of each piece of toast with mayonnaise and arrange the bacon, tomatoes and lettuce on top of two of the pieces. Season with salt and pepper and top with the other pieces of toast. Cut into quarters and serve hot or cold.

4 lean bacon rashers
4 slices of wholemeal bread or
   multi-grain bread
4 tablespoons mayonnaise
4 tomatoes, halved
about 8 baby lettuce leaves
salt and pepper

Serves **2**
Prep time **5 minutes**
Cooking time **10 minutes**

# SPICED
## MACKEREL FILLETS

2 tablespoons olive oil
1 tablespoon smoked paprika
1 teaspoon cayenne pepper
4 mackerel, scaled, filleted and
   pin-boned
2 limes, quartered
salt and pepper
rocket salad, to serve

Serves **4**
Prep time **4 minutes**
Cooking time **5-6 minutes**

**1** Mix together the oil, paprika and cayenne pepper with a little salt and pepper. Make three shallow cuts in the skin of the mackerel and brush over the spiced oil.

**2** Put the lime quarters and mackerel on a hot barbecue or griddle pan, skin side down first, and cook for 4-5 minutes until the skin is crispy and the limes are charred. Turn the fish over and cook for a further minute on the other side. Serve with a rocket salad.

# BRAISED POLLOCK
## *with lentils*

AFFORDABILITY
1

1   Boil the lentils in plenty of water for 15 minutes or according to the pack instructions. Drain and set aside.

2   Meanwhile, heat 1 tablespoon oil in a large frying pan, add the onion and fry for 5 minutes. Stir in the garlic and fry for a further 2 minutes.

3   Add the lentils, rosemary or thyme, stock and a little salt and pepper to the frying pan and bring to the boil.

4   Pour the mixture into a shallow, ovenproof dish and arrange the fish on top. Score the tops of the tomatoes and tuck them around the fish. Drizzle over the remaining oil and bake, uncovered, in a preheated oven, 180°C (350°F), Gas Mark 4, for 25 minutes or until the fish is cooked through. Serve sprinkled with the parsley.

150 g (5 oz) Puy lentils
3 tablespoons extra virgin olive oil
1 large onion, finely chopped
3 garlic cloves, sliced
several rosemary or thyme sprigs
200 ml (7 fl oz) Fish Stock (see page 235)
4 chunky pieces of pollock fillet, skinned
8 small tomatoes
salt and pepper
2 tablespoons chopped flat leaf parsley, to garnish

Serves **4**
Prep time **15 minutes**
Cooking time **50 minutes**

# TUNA & PASTA BAKE

300 g (10 oz) pasta shells
2 tablespoons olive oil
1 onion, finely chopped
2 red peppers, cored, deseeded
   and cubed
2 garlic cloves, crushed
200 g (7 oz) cherry tomatoes,
   halved
15 g (½ oz) butter
50 g (2 oz) fresh breadcrumbs
400 g (13 oz) can tuna, drained
   and flaked
125 g (4 oz) mozzarella or Gruyère
   cheese, grated

Serves **4**
Prep time **5 minutes**
Cooking time **15 minutes**

**1** Cook the pasta shells in a saucepan of lightly salted boiling water for 8-10 minutes or according to the pack instructions until just tender.

**2** Meanwhile, heat the oil in a large frying pan, add the onion and fry gently for 3 minutes. Add the peppers and garlic and fry, stirring frequently, for 5 minutes. Stir in the tomatoes and fry for 1 minute until they are soft.

**3** Melt the butter in another pan, toss in the breadcrumbs and stir until all the bread is covered in butter.

**4** Drain the pasta, add the pepper and tomato mix to the drained pasta and then stir in the tuna. Mix together and transfer to an ovenproof dish.

**5** Sprinkle the cheese and then the buttered breadcrumbs over the pasta and cook under a medium grill for 3-5 minutes until the cheese has melted and the breadcrumbs are golden.

# *Spicy* **TUNA** FISHCAKES

**1** Cook the potatoes in a large saucepan of lightly salted boiling water for 10 minutes or until tender. Drain well, mash and leave to cool slightly.

**2** Mix the tuna, cheese, spring onions, garlic, thyme and egg into the mashed potato. Season to taste with cayenne, salt and pepper.

**3** Divide the mixture into four and shape into thick patties. Season the flour with salt and pepper and dust the patties, then fry them in a shallow layer of vegetable oil for 5 minutes each side until crisp and golden. Serve hot with a mixed green salad and mayonnaise.

250 g (8 oz) floury potatoes, diced
2 x 200 g (7 oz) cans tuna in olive oil, drained and flaked
50 g (2 oz) Cheddar cheese, grated
4 spring onions, finely chopped
1 small garlic clove, crushed
2 teaspoons dried thyme
1 small egg, beaten
½ teaspoon cayenne pepper
60 g (2¼ oz) plain flour
salt and pepper
vegetable oil, for frying

**To serve**
mixed green salad
mayonnaise

Serves **4**
Prep time **10 minutes**
Cooking time **18 minutes**

### Ramp up reheat

Always reheat food thoroughly before you eat it. Leftover take-aways, in particular, have a serious reputation for rendering people incontinent and even hospital-bound. You should store leftovers in the refrigerator and heat thoroughly to kill any bugs that might be hiding. Don't reheat food more than once – if you haven't managed to eat it all in two sittings then you either ordered too much or it wasn't great quality in the first place.

# RED SALMON *&* ROASTED VEGETABLES

1 aubergine, cut into bite-sized
    pieces
2 red peppers, cored, deseeded
    and cut into bite-sized pieces
2 red onions, quartered
1 garlic clove, crushed
4 tablespoons olive oil
pinch of dried oregano
200 g (7 oz) can red salmon,
    drained and flaked
100 g (3½ oz) pitted black olives
salt and pepper
basil leaves, to garnish

Serves **4**
Prep time **10 minutes**
Cooking time **25 minutes**

**1** Mix together the aubergine, red peppers, onions and garlic in a bowl with the oil and oregano and season well with salt and pepper.

**2** Spread out the vegetables in a single layer in a nonstick roasting tin and roast in a preheated oven, 220°C (425°F), Gas Mark 7, for 25 minutes or until just cooked.

**3** Transfer the vegetables to a warm serving dish and gently toss in the salmon and olives. Garnish with basil leaves and serve warm or at room temperature.

# CREAMY TUNA & LEEK PASTA

1 Plunge the pasta into a large saucepan of lightly salted boiling water. Return to the boil and cook for 10-12 minutes or according to the pack instructions until just tender. Drain well and return to the pan.

2 Meanwhile, heat the oil in a frying pan, add the leeks, garlic and salt and pepper to taste and cook gently for 5 minutes.

3 Add the tuna and cook, stirring, for 1 minute. Add the wine, bring to the boil and boil until reduced by half. Stir in the cream and heat through for 2-3 minutes.

4 Add the tuna sauce to the pasta with the parsley and stir over a medium heat for 1 minute. Serve immediately with a rocket salad.

400 g (13 oz) dried penne
2 tablespoons extra virgin olive oil
2 leeks, sliced
2 large garlic cloves, sliced
2 x 200 g (7 oz) cans tuna in olive oil, drained and flaked
150 ml (¼ pint) dry white wine
150 ml (¼ pint) double cream
2 tablespoons chopped parsley
salt and pepper
rocket salad, to serve

Serves **4**
Prep time **10 minutes**
Cooking time **12 minutes**

AFFORDABILITY
1

# KEDGEREE

200 g (7 oz) smoked haddock
200 ml (7 fl oz) milk
1 bay leaf
2 teaspoons vegetable oil
1 small onion, chopped
125 g (4 oz) basmati rice
½ teaspoon curry powder
2 hard-boiled eggs, roughly
    chopped
1 tablespoon chopped parsley

Serves **2**
Prep time **10 minutes**
Cooking time **15 minutes**

**1** Put the haddock in a small saucepan with the milk and bay leaf, simmer for 3 minutes or until just cooked and remove the fish, reserving the milk. Flake the fish and set aside.

**2** Heat the oil in a frying pan, add the onion and fry for 3 minutes. Add the rice and curry powder, stir and fry for a further minute.

**3** Make up the reserved milk to 250 ml (8 fl oz) with water and pour it over the rice. Cover and cook for 12 minutes until the rice is cooked and fluffy. Add the remaining ingredients and the flaked haddock, stir to combine and serve.

AFFORDABILITY
1

# MUSHROOM STROGANOFF

AFFORDABILITY
1

1 Melt the butter with the oil in a large frying pan, add the onion and garlic and cook until soft and starting to brown.

2 Add the mushrooms to the pan and cook until soft and starting to brown. Stir in the mustard and crème fraîche and just heat through. Season to taste with salt and pepper, then serve immediately, garnished with the chopped parsley.

15 g (½ oz) butter
2 tablespoons olive oil
1 onion, thinly sliced
4 garlic cloves, finely chopped
500 g (1 lb) chestnut mushrooms,
  sliced
2 tablespoons wholegrain mustard
250 ml (8 fl oz) crème fraîche
salt and pepper
3 tablespoons chopped parsley, to
  garnish

Serves **4**
Prep time **10 minutes**
Cooking time **10 minutes**

# SWEETCORN & PEPPER *Frittata*

2 tablespoons olive oil
4 spring onions, thinly sliced
200 g (7 oz) can sweetcorn, drained
150 g (5 oz) ready-roasted red peppers in oil, drained and cut into strips
4 eggs, lightly beaten
125 g (4 oz) strong Cheddar cheese, grated
small handful of chives, finely chopped
salt and pepper

**To serve**
green salad
crusty bread

Serves **4**
Prep time **10 minutes**
Cooking time **10 minutes**

**1** Heat the oil in a frying pan with a flameproof handle, add the spring onions, sweetcorn and red peppers and cook for 30 seconds.

**2** Add the eggs, cheese and chives, season to taste with salt and pepper and cook over a medium heat for 4–5 minutes until the base is set. Remove from the hob and place under a preheated grill and cook for 3–4 minutes or until golden and set.

**3** Cut into wedges and serve immediately with a green salad and crusty bread.

# CAULIFLOWER CHEESE

1 large cauliflower, divided into
  florets
25 g (1 oz) butter
25 g (1 oz) plain flour
300 ml (½ pint) milk
125 g (4 oz) Cheddar cheese,
  grated
1 teaspoon Dijon mustard
1 tablespoon fresh breadcrumbs
salt and pepper
4 grilled back bacon rashers, cut
  into strips, to garnish

Serves **4**
Prep time **10 minutes**
Cooking time **15 minutes**

**1** Steam the cauliflower over a pan of lightly salted boiling water for about 12 minutes until tender. Drain and transfer to an ovenproof dish.

**2** Meanwhile, melt the butter in a heavy-based saucepan, stir in the flour and cook for 1 minute. Slowly stir in the milk, then two-thirds of the Cheddar and heat. Stir constantly, until the sauce has thickened. Season with mustard, salt and pepper.

**3** Pour the sauce over the cauliflower, sprinkle with the remaining cheese and scatter the breadcrumbs over the top. Cook under a medium grill until the top is golden brown. Garnish with bacon strips.

AFFORDABILITY
1

# INDIVIDUAL MACARONI CHEESES

1 Cook the macaroni in a large saucepan of lightly salted boiling water for 10-12 minutes or according to the pack instructions until just tender. Drain and place in a large bowl.

2 Meanwhile, dry-fry the bacon in a small frying pan until browned but not crisp. Add the garlic, fry for 1 minute and then add the cream and milk and season with a little nutmeg. Bring just to boiling point.

3 Stir in 125 g (4 oz) cheese and all the basil, remove from the heat and stir until the cheese melts. Season to taste with salt and pepper and stir into the macaroni.

4 Spoon into individual gratin dishes, top with the remaining cheese and bake in a preheated oven, 230°C (450°F), Gas Mark 8, for 10 minutes, until golden.

250 g (8 oz) macaroni
4 rashers smoked back bacon, diced
1 garlic clove, crushed
150 ml (¼ pint) single cream
150 ml (¼ pint) milk
pinch of grated nutmeg
175 g (6 oz) hard cheese, such as Cheddar or Gruyère, grated
4 tablespoons chopped basil
salt and pepper

Serves **4**
Prep time **5 minutes**
Cooking time **20 minutes**

3 tablespoons sunflower oil
300 g (10 oz) firm tofu, cubed
1 onion, sliced
2 carrots, sliced
150 g (5 oz) broccoli, broken
  into small florets and stalks
  sliced
1 red pepper, cored, deseeded
  and sliced
1 large courgette, sliced
150 g (5 oz) sugar snap peas
2 tablespoons soy sauce
2 tablespoons sweet chilli
  sauce

**To garnish**
chopped red chillies
Thai or ordinary basil leaves

Serves **4**
Prep time **10 minutes**
Cooking time **7 minutes**

# **VEGETABLE** & TOFU STIR-FRY

**1** Heat 1 tablespoon of oil in a wok or large frying pan until it starts to smoke, add the tofu and stir-fry over a high heat for 2 minutes until golden. Remove from the pan with a slotted spoon.

**2** Heat the remaining oil in the pan, add the onion and carrots and stir-fry for 1½ minutes. Add the broccoli and red pepper and stir-fry for 1 minute, then add the courgette and sugar snap peas and stir-fry for 1 minute.

**3** Mix the soy and chilli sauces with 125 ml (4 fl oz) water and add to the pan with the tofu. Cook for 1 minute. Serve in bowls, garnished with chopped red chillies and basil leaves.

# STIR-FRIED
## VEGETABLE
### *Noodles*

1 Cook the noodles in a large saucepan of lightly salted boiling water for about 4 minutes or until just tender. Drain.

2 Heat the oil in a large frying pan or wok, add the spring onions and carrots and stir-fry for 3 minutes. Add the garlic, chilli flakes, mangetout and mushrooms and stir-fry for 2 minutes. Add the Chinese leaves and stir-fry for 1 minute.

3 Add the drained noodles to the pan with the soy sauce and hoisin sauce. Stir-fry over a gentle heat for 2 minutes until heated through and serve immediately.

250 g (8 oz) egg noodles
4 tablespoons groundnut oil
1 bunch of spring onions, sliced
2 carrots, thinly sliced
2 garlic cloves, crushed
¼ teaspoon dried chilli flakes
125 g (4 oz) mangetout
125 g (4 oz) shiitake mushrooms, halved
3 Chinese leaves, shredded
2 tablespoons light soy sauce
3 tablespoons hoisin sauce

Serves **4**
Prep time **10 minutes**
Cooking time **12 minutes**

# Herb Omelette
## WITH MUSTARD
# MUSHROOMS

IF YOU PREFER, COOK HALF THE EGG MIXTURE AT A TIME TO MAKE TWO SMALLER OMELETTES.

1 tablespoon wholegrain mustard
50 g (2 oz) butter, softened
4 flat mushrooms
2 tablespoons chopped mixed
  herbs (such as chives, parsley
  and tarragon)
4 eggs
salt and pepper

Serves **2**
Prep time **5 minutes**
Cooking time **10 minutes**

**1** Beat the mustard into 40 g (1½ oz) butter and spread over the undersides of the mushrooms. Place on a foil-lined grill pan and cook for 5-6 minutes until golden and tender. Remove and keep warm.

**2** Meanwhile, beat the herbs into the eggs and season to taste with salt and pepper.

**3** Melt the remaining butter in an omelette or nonstick frying pan, swirl in the egg mixture and cook until almost set. Carefully slide and flip over on to a warmed plate, add the mushrooms and serve.

### Bottle it up

It's worth keeping a few glass jars and lids in the kitchen. They're handy for mixing up salad dressings or sauces. Alternatively, if you're going for a hippy chick look for your next gathering, pop a tea light or small bunch of flowers (or pretty weeds, if gardening isn't your forte) inside for table decorations.

AFFORDABILITY
1

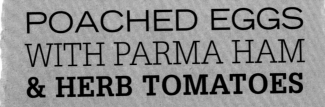

# POACHED EGGS WITH PARMA HAM & HERB TOMATOES

AFFORDABILITY 2

THIS IS A HEALTHIER VERSION OF THE TRADITIONAL 'FRY-UP'.

1 Halve the tomatoes and place them, cut side up, on a foil-lined grill pan. Mix the basil with 2 tablespoons oil and drizzle over the tomatoes. Season well with salt and pepper. Cook under a preheated grill for 6-7 minutes until softened. Remove and keep warm.

2 Meanwhile, heat the remaining oil in a frying pan and fry the ham until crisp. Drain on kitchen paper and keep warm.

3 Poach the eggs in gently simmering water or an egg poacher for 3-4 minutes. Serve on buttered toasted muffins with the ham and grilled tomatoes.

4 ripe tomatoes
2 tablespoons chopped basil
4 tablespoons extra virgin olive oil
4 slices of Parma ham
4 large eggs
salt and pepper
hot buttered muffins, to serve

Serves **4**
Prep time **5 minutes**
Cooking time **10-12 minutes**

**AFFORDABILITY 1**

# POTATO TORTILLA

150 ml (¼ pint) extra virgin olive oil
750 g (1½ lb) waxy potatoes, thinly sliced
1 onion, chopped
1 red pepper, sliced
1 green pepper, sliced
5 eggs, beaten
salt and pepper

Serves **6**
Prep time **10 minutes**
Cooking time **30–35 minutes**

1 Heat all but 2 tablespoons of the oil in a large nonstick frying pan and fry the potatoes, onion and peppers, stirring frequently, for 15 minutes, until all the vegetables are golden and tender.

2 Mix the potato mixture with the eggs in a large bowl and season well with salt and pepper. Set aside for 15 minutes. Clean the frying pan.

3 Heat the remaining oil in the clean pan and tip in the tortilla mixture. Cook over a low heat for 10 minutes, until almost cooked through. Carefully slide the tortilla onto a large plate, invert the frying pan over the tortilla and then flip it back into the frying pan.

4 Return the pan to the heat and cook the tortilla for a further 5 minutes, or until it is cooked on both sides. Leave to cool, then serve at room temperature, cut into wedges.

# CANNELLINI BEANS ON TOAST

1 Heat the oil in a saucepan, add the onion and celery and fry for 5 minutes until golden. Blend the cornflour with 2 tablespoons water and add to the pan with the remaining ingredients.

2 Bring to the boil, reduce the heat slightly and season to taste with salt and pepper. Cook, uncovered, for about 20 minutes, stirring frequently, until the mixture is thick and pulpy. Pile on toast to serve.

2 tablespoons groundnut or vegetable oil
1 onion, chopped
1 celery stick, thinly sliced
1 teaspoon cornflour
425 g (14 oz) can cannellini beans
250 g (8 oz) can chopped tomatoes
300 ml (½ pint) Vegetable Stock (see page 235)
1 tablespoon coarse-grain mustard
1 tablespoon black treacle
1 tablespoon tomato ketchup
1 tablespoon Worcestershire sauce
salt and pepper
toasted chunky bread, to serve

Serves **2-3**
Prep time **5 minutes**
Cooking time **25 minutes**

# RATATOUILLE

125 ml (4 fl oz) olive oil
2 large aubergines, quartered lengthways and cut into 1 cm (½ inch) slices
2 courgettes, cut into 1 cm (½ inch) slices
2 large red peppers, cored, deseeded and cut into squares
1 large yellow pepper, cored, deseeded and cut into squares
2 large onions, thinly sliced
3 large garlic cloves, crushed
2 tablespoons tomato purée
400 g (13 oz) can plum tomatoes
12 basil leaves, chopped
1 tablespoon finely chopped marjoram or oregano
1 teaspoon finely chopped thyme
1 tablespoon paprika
2-4 tablespoons finely chopped parsley
salt and pepper

Serves **8**
Prep time **10 minutes**
Cooking time **30 minutes**

1 Heat half the oil in a roasting tin in a preheated oven, 220°C (425°F), Gas Mark 7. Add the aubergines, courgettes and peppers and toss in the hot oil, return to the oven and roast for about 30 minutes or until tender.

2 Meanwhile, heat the remaining oil in a deep saucepan, add the onions and garlic and cook over a medium heat for 3-5 minutes until softened but not browned. Add the tomato purée, plum tomatoes, herbs and paprika and season to taste with salt and pepper. Stir to combine, then cook for 10-15 minutes until the mixture is thick and syrupy.

3 Use a slotted spoon to transfer the vegetables from the roasting tin to the tomato mixture. Gently stir to combine, then add the parsley and adjust the seasoning if necessary. Serve hot or cold with crusty bread or as an accompaniment to meats or poultry.

# POTATO WEDGES & PEPPERS WITH YOGURT DIP

1 Cut the potato into eight wedges. Bring a saucepan of lightly salted water to the boil, add the potato wedges and cook for 5 minutes. Drain the wedges thoroughly and put them in a bowl with the red pepper slices and oil. Toss well to mix. Sprinkle with paprika and rock salt to taste.

2 Put the potato wedges and pepper slices on a baking sheet and cook under a preheated hot grill, turning occasionally, for 6-8 minutes until lightly browned and tender.

3 Meanwhile, make the yogurt dip. In a bowl mix together all the ingredients and season to taste with salt and pepper.

4 Serve the potato wedges and pepper slices hot with the yogurt dip.

1 potato, about 175 g (6 oz), scrubbed
1 red pepper, cored, deseeded and sliced
1 teaspoon olive oil
paprika
rock salt

**Yogurt dip**
3 tablespoons Greek yogurt
1 tablespoon chopped parsley
2 spring onions, chopped
1 garlic clove, crushed (optional)
salt and pepper

Serves **2**
Prep time **15 minutes**
Cooking time **15 minutes**

### Bag it up

Next time you go to the supermarket, stock up on a few packs of freezer bags. They take up less space in the cupboard than plastic containers and they're ideal for freezing leftover portions of sauces, curries etc. Use a marker pen to stake your claim to your culinary masterpieces and lay them flat in the freezer drawer.

AFFORDABILITY
1

# EAT
## HEALTHY

AUBERGINE & POTATO CAKES

CHICKPEAS WITH CHORIZO

THREE PEPPER SALAD

DUCK TACOS

AFFORDABILITY
2

**Nutrient analysis per serving**

| 1549 kJ | 371 kcal | energy |
|---|---|---|
| | 33.3 g | protein |
| | 15.2 g | carbohydrate |
| | 7.6 g | sugars |
| | 20.0 g | fat |
| | 4.1 g | saturates |
| | 3.3 g | fibre |
| | 268 mg | sodium |

# CHICKEN & CASHEW NUTS
# WITH VEGETABLES

250 ml (8 fl oz) Chicken Stock (see
 page 234)
400 g (13 oz) boneless, skinless
 chicken breast, cubed
2 tablespoons ready-made yellow
 bean sauce
200 g (7 oz) carrots, sliced
200 g (7 oz) bamboo shoots,
 sliced
200 g (7 oz) cashew nuts, toasted
1 spring onion, shredded

**Cornflour paste**
1 teaspoon cornflour
2 tablespoons water or stock

Serves **4**
Prep time **15 minutes**
Cooking time **15 minutes**

1 Put the stock in a saucepan and bring to the boil. Add
 the chicken meat and bring the liquid back to boil,
stirring. Lower the heat and cook for 5 minutes. Remove
the chicken with a slotted spoon and set aside.

2 Add the yellow bean sauce and cook for a couple of
 minutes. Add the carrots and bamboo shoots and
cook for another couple of minutes.

3 Make the cornflour paste. Mix the cornflour with the
 water or stock to make a smooth, lump-free paste.

4 Return the chicken to the pan, bring the sauce back
 to boil and thicken with cornflour paste. Stir in the
cashew nuts and spring onion just before serving. Serve
with rice, if liked.

# CHICKEN, COUSCOUS
## *&* ONIONS

**1** Put the chicken in a large saucepan, add 750 ml (1¼ pints) water and bring slowly to the boil. Add the bouquet garni, onion, garlic, saffron and 1¼ teaspoons of salt. Reduce the heat, cover and simmer for 50-60 minutes until the chicken is tender. Add the ginger and pepper 5 minutes before the end of cooking.

**2** Meanwhile, put the couscous in a bowl and cover it with water. Rake it through with your fingers, then drain and immediately spread it evenly over a large tray. Rake the grains with your fingers a few times to aerate them, then leave for 20-30 minutes until the water is absorbed and the couscous is relatively dry.

**3** Rub the couscous gently between your palms, letting it fall back into the tray, to break down any lumps. Sprinkle with the remaining salt, drizzle over 1 tablespoon of the oil and rake through the grains again.

**4** Ladle 300 ml (½ pint) stock from the large pan into a small pan and bring to a rapid boil, turn off the heat and add the couscous. Cover and leave until the stock has been absorbed.

**5** Heat the remaining oil in a pan, add the onions and fry gently until lightly golden. Ladle 200 ml (7 fl oz) stock into a small bowl. Pour a little stock over the onions and cook until reduced. Repeat until all the stock has been added and reduced. As the onions soften, increase the heat.

**6** Add the raisins, cinnamon and nutmeg, then the honey and leave to caramelize for 5-10 minutes. Stir in the flower water or rosewater, if using, and turn off the heat.

**7** Transfer the couscous to a serving dish and top with the onions. Serve the chicken and stock separately.

1 small chicken, cut into 6-8 pieces
bouquet garni (1 cinnamon stick, 1 bay leaf, 1 cardamom pod, tied together with string)
1 onion, finely chopped
3 garlic cloves, crushed
generous pinch of saffron threads
1½ teaspoons salt
½ teaspoon ground ginger
¼ teaspoon black pepper
250 g (8 oz) couscous
2 tablespoons extra virgin olive oil
500 g (1 lb) onions, sliced
75 g (3 oz) raisins
½ teaspoon ground cinnamon
small pinch of grated nutmeg
1-2 tablespoons dark honey
scant ½ tablespoon orange flower water or rosewater (optional)

Serves **4-6**
Prep time **1 hour**
Cooking time **1½ hours**

**Nutrient analysis per serving**

| 3256 kJ | 780 kcal | energy |
|---|---|---|
| | 46 g | protein |
| | 66 g | carbohydrate |
| | 32 g | sugars |
| | 39 g | fat |
| | 9 g | saturates |
| | 3 g | fibre |
| | 0.7 g | sodium |

# DUCK TACOS

AFFORDABILITY
**3**

1.75 kg (3½ lb) hot roasted duck
16 40 g (1½ oz) soft corn tortillas
1 onion, finely chopped
8 green chillies, chopped
  (deseeded for a milder taste)
30 g (1 oz) fresh coriander, finely
  chopped
salt
finely chopped tomato, to garnish
  (optional)
salsa of your choice, to serve

Serves **4**
Prep time **20 minutes**
Cooking time **6-8 minutes**

**1** Shred the hot roasted duck meat, discarding any fat, and keep warm.

**2** Preheat a large, dry, heavy-based frying pan over a medium heat, warm each side of the tortillas, two or three at a time, for about 30 seconds in the hot pan until soft. Transfer to a basket and cover with a clean tea towel.

**3** Put about 20 g (¾ oz) of shredded duck on top of one warm tortilla, scatter some of the onion, chillies and coriander on top, season with salt to taste, roll up and place on a warm platter. Cover with the clean tea towel. Repeat with the remaining ingredients.

**4** Serve immediately with your favourite salsa and garnish with chopped tomato, if liked.

## Healthy tip

DUCK CAN BE HIGH IN FAT, SO ALWAYS REMOVE THE SKIN AND AS MUCH FAT AS POSSIBLE TO MAKE THIS NUTRITIOUS DISH HEALTHIER.

## Nutrient analysis per serving

| 3430 kJ | 816 kcal | energy |
|---|---|---|
| | 54 g | protein |
| | 93 g | carbohydrate |
| | 2 g | sugars |
| | 25 g | fat |
| | 4 g | saturates |
| | 5 g | fibre |
| | 570 mg | sodium |

# SAVOURY MEATBALLS

300 g (10 oz) minced pork
3 garlic cloves, crushed
50 g (2 oz) dried white
  breadcrumbs
1 teaspoon ground cumin
1 teaspoon ground coriander
1 teaspoon ground nutmeg
1 teaspoon ground cinnamon
2 tablespoons olive oil
salt and pepper

**Sauce**
1 tablespoon olive oil
1 small onion, finely chopped
1 garlic clove, crushed
400 g (13 oz) can chopped
  tomatoes
1 teaspoon golden caster sugar
1 teaspoon mild paprika
100 g (3½ oz) fresh or frozen peas

Makes **about 30**
Prep time **20 minutes, plus
chilling**
Cooking time **40-50 minutes**

1 Put the minced meat, garlic, breadcrumbs and spices in a bowl. Season to taste with salt and pepper. Use your fingers to mix thoroughly. Cover and chill in the refrigerator for 1 hour.

2 Meanwhile, make the sauce. Heat the oil in a large frying pan, cook the onion and garlic over a medium heat, stirring frequently, for 5-6 minutes. Stir in the tomatoes, sugar and paprika, bring to the boil. Reduce the heat, cover and simmer gently, stirring occasionally, for 25-30 minutes. Add the peas, season to taste with salt and pepper and cook for 2-3 minutes.

3 Shape walnut-sized pieces of the minced meat mixture into balls. Heat half the oil in a nonstick frying pan and cook half the meatballs over a medium heat, stirring, for 2-3 minutes until browned all over. Remove with a slotted spoon and drain on kitchen paper. Repeat with the remaining oil and meatballs.

4 Add the meatballs to the sauce over a medium heat, stir to coat evenly, then simmer gently for 5-6 minutes. Serve hot.

### Nutrient analysis per serving

| 1122 kJ | 266 kcal | energy |
|---|---|---|
| | 20 g | protein |
| | 15 g | carbohydrate |
| | 6 g | sugars |
| | 15 g | fat |
| | 3 g | saturates |
| | 3 g | fibre |
| | 164 mg | sodium |

# GRILLED PORK STEAKS WITH SAGE

1 Using a sharp knife, cut a horizontal pocket through the centre of each pork steak.

2 Mix together the garlic, sage and oil and rub this mixture all over the outside and inside of the pork steaks. Place in a dish, cover and leave to marinate in the refrigerator for at least 30 minutes or overnight.

3 Season the outside and inside of the pork steaks with salt and pepper and place them on a foil-lined baking sheet. Cook under a preheated hot grill, about 10 cm (4 inches) from the heat, for 5 minutes. Turn over the steaks and cook for a further 5 minutes or until cooked through and golden.

4 pork loin steaks, about 200 g (7 oz) each
2 garlic cloves, finely chopped
1½ tablespoons finely chopped sage
1 teaspoon olive oil
salt and pepper

Serves **4**
Prep time **15 minutes, plus marinating**
Cooking time **10 minutes**

## Healthy tip

PORK USED TO BE A VERY FATTY MEAT, BUT TODAY PIGS ARE BRED TO BE MUCH LEANER. THERE IS STILL A CERTAIN AMOUNT OF INVISIBLE FAT INCORPORATED IN THE LEAN MEAT, WHICH HELPS GIVE PORK ITS TEXTURE AND FLAVOUR, SO TRIM ANY VISIBLE FAT OFF TO KEEP THE MEAT AS LEAN AS POSSIBLE.

## Nutrient analysis per serving

| 1280 kJ | 306 kcal | energy |
|---|---|---|
| | 42 g | protein |
| | 1 g | carbohydrate |
| | 0 g | sugars |
| | 15 g | fat |
| | 5 g | saturates |
| | 0 g | fibre |
| | 74 mg | sodium |

AFFORDABILITY 1

# CHICKPEAS
## WITH CHORIZO

2 tablespoons olive oil
1 red onion, finely chopped
2 garlic cloves, crushed
200 g (7 oz) chorizo sausage, cut into 1 cm (½ inch) dice
2 ripe tomatoes, deseeded and finely chopped
3 tablespoons chopped flat leaf parsley
2 x 400 g (13 oz) cans chickpeas in water, rinsed and drained
salt and pepper

Serves **4**
Prep time **10 minutes**
Cooking time **10 minutes**

1 Heat the oil in a large, nonstick frying pan, add the onion, garlic and chorizo and cook over a medium-high heat, stirring frequently, for 4-5 minutes.

2 Add the tomatoes, parsley and chickpeas to the pan and cook, stirring frequently, for 4-5 minutes until heated through. Season to taste with salt and pepper and serve immediately or leave to cool to room temperature.

## Healthy tip

CHICKPEAS ARE NOT ONLY A GREAT SOURCE OF DIETARY FIBRE, THEY ALSO CONTAIN IRON, WHICH IS ESSENTIAL FOR HEALTHY BLOOD. THE VITAMIN C FROM THE TOMATOES IN THIS DISH WILL HELP IN THE ABSORPTION OF THE IRON.

### Nutrient analysis per serving

| 1737 kJ | 415 kcal | energy |
|---|---|---|
| | 24 g | protein |
| | 36 g | carbohydrate |
| | 7 g | sugars |
| | 21 g | fat |
| | 6 g | saturates |
| | 10 g | fibre |
| | 300 mg | sodium |

# ROASTED SEA BASS
## WITH **POTATOES**
### & WILD MUSHROOMS

IF FRESH WILD MUSHROOMS ARE NOT AVAILABLE, USE A COMBINATION OF DRIED PORCINI AND CULTIVATED MUSHROOMS, REDUCING THE SOAKING LIQUID FROM THE PORCINI AND ADDING IT TO THE POTATOES WITH THE MUSHROOMS.

875 g (1¾ lb) potatoes, peeled
2 garlic cloves, thinly sliced
3 tablespoons olive oil
250 g (8 oz) mixed wild
  mushrooms, sliced if large
4 sea bass fillets, about 175 g
  (6 oz) each
½ tablespoon chopped flat leaf
  parsley
extra virgin olive oil, for drizzling
salt and pepper

Serves **4**
Prep time **15 minutes**
Cooking time **35-40 minutes**

1 Peel the potatoes, cut them into slices about 1 cm (½ inch) thick and put them in a large roasting tin lined with greaseproof paper. Stir in half the garlic and 2 tablespoons olive oil and season with salt and pepper. Spread out the potatoes in a single layer and roast in a preheated oven, 240°C (475°F), Gas Mark 9, for 18-20 minutes or until cooked through and golden.

2 Meanwhile, heat ½ tablespoon of the remaining olive oil in a frying pan over a high heat, add the mushrooms and the remaining garlic and cook, stirring frequently, until just tender. Season with salt and pepper.

3 Stir the cooked mushrooms into the roasted potatoes. Season the sea bass fillets and place them, skin side up, on top of the potatoes. Scatter with the parsley and drizzle the fish with the remaining olive oil. Roast for 10-12 minutes until the fish is cooked through. Serve immediately with a drizzle of extra virgin olive oil.

## Healthy tip

SEA BASS IS A LOW FAT FISH THAT PROVIDES USEFUL AMOUNTS OF VITAMIN A AND SELENIUM (THOUGHT TO AID IN THE PREVENTION OF CANCER).

### Nutrient analysis per serving

| | | |
|---|---|---|
| 1839 kJ | 438 kcal | energy |
| | 40 g | protein |
| | 38 g | carbohydrate |
| | 2 g | sugars |
| | 15 g | fat |
| | 2 g | saturates |
| | 5 g | fibre |
| | 140 mg | sodium |

# BENGALI-STYLE
# MUSTARD FISH

1 Use a mortar and pestle to crush the turmeric, chilli powder, wholegrain mustard and black mustard seeds until fairly well combined. Add the oil and lime juice and season well. Stir to mix thoroughly.

2 Line a baking sheet with nonstick baking paper and put the fish fillets on the baking sheet. Spread the mustard mixture over the fish and cook in a preheated oven, 200°C (400°F), Gas Mark 6, for 15-20 minutes or until cooked through. Remove from the oven and serve immediately, garnished with chopped coriander.

1 teaspoon turmeric
1 teaspoon chilli powder
2 tablespoons wholegrain mustard
2 teaspoons black mustard seeds
2 tablespoons sunflower oil
juice of 1 lime
salt
4 thick halibut or cod fillets, each about 250 g (8 oz), skinned
chopped fresh coriander leaves, to garnish

Serves **4**
Prep time **10 minutes**
Cooking time **15-20 minutes**

## Something fishy

Fish is ultra-healthy and easy to cook, but it doesn't often feature on student dinner menus. For a fuss-free fish supper drizzle some olive oil into a large square of kitchen foil, place the fish fillet on top and add a lemon slice and any herbs you have lying around. Make the foil into a loose, sealed parcel around the fish and cook for 12–15 minutes (depending on size). The fish will be moist and the kitchen won't smell. Perfect!

AFFORDABILITY
3

### Nutrient analysis per serving

| | | |
|---|---|---|
| 958 kJ | 228 kcal | energy |
| | 32 g | protein |
| | 1 g | carbohydrate |
| | 0 g | sugars |
| | 11 g | fat |
| | 1 g | saturates |
| | 0 g | fibre |
| | 274 mg | sodium |

# TREAT YOUR
# BODY
## LIKE A TEMPLE

If you think you can get your five a day from a steady diet of vodka and orange you're going to have to re-think your eating habits. That's not to say that vodka has to be banished entirely – you just need to shuffle the proportions to make way for healthy additions. It is possible to eat well and to still have a few coppers left over for happy hour.

## IRON IT OUT

You need iron to keep your blood bubbling away happily. If you're a carnivore you'll have no problems stocking up. However, if you shy away from steak, you should nibble nuts, dried fruit and plenty of green vegetables.

## FORTY WINKS

Mid-week all nighters are inevitable but try to squeeze in a regular 8 hours'

| Suggestions for your five a day | Portion size |
| --- | --- |
| Orange juice with breakfast | 150 ml (¼ pint) glass |
| Chopped fruit on cereal | a handful of grapes or 7 strawberries |
| Fruit snack | apple, banana, orange, pear etc |
| Salad snack | 1 tomato, 3 celery sticks or a handful of cherry tomatoes |
| Dried fruit | 1 tablespoon |
| Vegetable portion | 2 broccoli florets, 3 tablespoons cooked peas, sweetcorn or carrots |

## FIGHTING FIT

Protein helps your body to heal itself and grow so it should be muscling in on most of your meals. Chicken, eggs, dairy produce, fish and grains are all good sources, so it shouldn't be too taxing to find ways of putting protein on your plate.

## ENERGY FOOD

As well as plenty of fruit and vegetables, you should try to include 'good' carbohydrates in your diet. By 'good' we're talking about the slow burners that will release energy gradually and keep you feeling full. Wholemeal or granary bread, pasta, rice and potatoes are all good, cheap sources of carbohydrates, and these should have a big presence on the dinner table.

## STRETCH YOUR LEGS

Running for a lecture after you've overslept or bed-hopping your way around the campus might supply sporadic bouts of exercise, but you really should include some kind of regular sporting activity in your weekly schedule. Let's face it: if you can't find the time for a quick game of footie or a step class when you're at uni then you never will.

The choices you make now regarding your diet and lifestyle can have long-term implications. At the risk of sounding like your mum, you need to make sure you eat properly and look after yourself. That means eating regular, healthy meals (rather than replacing solid food with a liquid diet) and getting fresh air and exercise. Student halls are worse than medieval London for the rapid spread of every contagious illness known to mankind, and your best chance of avoiding flu, endless colds and other nasty bugs related to communal living is to boost your immune system with a balanced diet.

# TRADITIONAL
# FISH & POTATO
# STEW

AFFORDABILITY
3

800 g (1 lb 10 oz) tuna fillets, cut
  into large bite-sized pieces
4 tablespoons olive oil
2 red onions, halved and thinly
  sliced
4 garlic cloves, thinly sliced
3 ripe tomatoes, skinned,
  deseeded and chopped
2 bay leaves
1 red pepper, cored, deseeded and
  diced
1 tablespoon mild paprika
625 g (1¼ lb) potatoes, peeled and
  cut into large bite-sized pieces
salt and pepper

**To garnish**
chopped flat leaf parsley
capers

Serves **4**
Prep time **15 minutes**
Cooking time **40-45 minutes**

1 Arrange the tuna in a shallow bowl in a single layer and
season to taste with salt and pepper. Cover and set aside.

2 Heat the oil in a saucepan, add the onions and garlic
and cook over a medium heat, stirring frequently, for
8-10 minutes until soft.

3 Add the tomatoes, bay leaves, red pepper, paprika and
potatoes and stir to mix well. Add enough water to just
cover all the ingredients and bring to the boil. Reduce the heat
and simmer gently for 25-30 minutes or until the potatoes are
tender. Add the fish, return to the boil and cook for 4-5 minutes.

4 Taste and adjust the seasoning if necessary and serve
ladled into warmed shallow bowls and garnished with
chopped parsley and capers.

## Healthy tip

TUNA IS AN EXCELLENT, LOW FAT
SOURCE OF PROTEIN. THE
COMBINATION OF TUNA WITH
POTATOES, TOMATOES AND
ONIONS MAKES THIS A
PARTICULARLY NUTRITIOUS DISH.

### Nutrient analysis per serving

| 2299 kJ | 547 kcal | energy |
|---|---|---|
| | 53 g | protein |
| | 39 g | carbohydrate |
| | 11 g | sugars |
| | 21 g | fat |
| | 4 g | saturates |
| | 6 g | fibre |
| | 119 mg | sodium |

# *Pumpkin* CURRY

**1** Put the pumpkin or butternut squash in a saucepan with the turmeric, paprika and 750 ml (1¼ pints) water. Bring to the boil and simmer gently for 6–8 minutes or until tender.

**2** Grind half the coconut in a spice mill or a mortar and pestle with the cumin seeds. Stir this into the pumpkin mixture and stir and cook for 2–3 minutes. Remove from the heat.

**3** Heat the oil in a small, nonstick frying pan, add the mustard seeds, curry leaves and red chillies, stir and cook over a high heat for 1–2 minutes. Tip this mixture over the pumpkin curry. Season to taste and serve.

500 g (1 lb) pumpkin or butternut squash, cut into 2.5 cm (1 inch) cubes
1 teaspoon turmeric
1 teaspoon smoked paprika
200 g (7 oz) freshly grated coconut
1 teaspoon cumin seeds
1 tablespoon sunflower oil
1 teaspoon black mustard seeds
8–10 curry leaves
2 small red chillies, split in half lengthways
salt and pepper

Serves **4**
Prep time **10 minutes**
Cooking time **10–13 minutes**

AFFORDABILITY **1**

## Nutrient analysis per serving

| 976 kJ | 236 kcal | energy |
|---|---|---|
| | 3 g | protein |
| | 7 g | carbohydrate |
| | 4 g | sugars |
| | 22 g | fat |
| | 16 g | saturates |
| | 7 g | fibre |
| | 12 mg | sodium |

## Healthy tip

ORANGE-FLESHED VEGETABLES ARE AN EXCELLENT SOURCE OF THE IMMUNE-BOOSTING NUTRIENT BETA-CAROTENE.

# CHICKPEA CURRY

AFFORDABILITY
1

1 tablespoon sunflower oil
2 garlic cloves, crushed
1 teaspoon finely grated fresh root
  ginger
2 tablespoons medium or hot
  curry powder
400 g (13 oz) can chopped
  tomatoes
1 teaspoon grated jaggery or palm
  sugar
2 x 400 g (13 oz) cans chickpeas,
  rinsed and drained
salt
low-fat yogurt, to drizzle
small handful of chopped fresh
  coriander leaves, to garnish

Serves **4**
Prep time **10 minutes**
Cooking time **13-15 minutes**

**1** Heat the oil in a large, nonstick wok or frying pan, add the garlic and ginger and stir-fry for 30 seconds. Add the curry powder, stir and cook for 1 minute, then add the chopped tomatoes and jaggery or palm sugar. Bring the mixture to the boil, cover, reduce the heat and cook over a medium heat for 10-12 minutes.

**2** Stir in the chickpeas and mix well. Cook over a medium heat for 3-4 minutes. Season, remove from the heat.

**3** Drizzle with low-fat yogurt and sprinkle over chopped coriander before serving.

## Nutrient analysis per serving

| 1232 kJ | 292 kcal | energy |
|---|---|---|
| | 16 g | protein |
| | 39 g | carbohydrate |
| | 5 g | sugars |
| | 9 g | fat |
| | 1 g | saturates |
| | 1 g | fibre |
| | 503 mg | sodium |

### Healthy tip

PULSES SUCH AS CHICKPEAS CONTAIN USEFUL AMOUNTS OF B VITAMINS, IRON, CALCIUM AND FIBRE. THEY ARE ALSO A GOOD SOURCE OF COMPLEX CARBOHYDRATES, WHICH PROVIDE A STEADY STREAM OF ENERGY.

# **HUEVOS** RANCHEROS

1 Make the sauce. Put the tomatoes, onion, garlic and chillies in a blender or food processor and blend to until the mixture is a fairly smooth texture.

2 Heat the oil in a saucepan set over a medium heat, add the tomato mixture and simmer, stirring constantly, for about 10 minutes or until cooked. Add salt to taste and keep warm until required.

3 Preheat a large, dry, heavy-based frying pan over a medium heat. Brush the tortillas with oil and warm each side of two tortillas at a time in the hot pan for about 30 seconds until soft. Cover with kitchen foil to keep warm.

4 Preheat a dry, nonstick frying pan over a medium heat. Break the eggs, two at a time, into the pan and cook over a low heat until the whites have set.

5 Put one tortilla on each plate and place two cooked eggs on top. Spoon the sauce generously over the whites of the eggs, leaving the yolks exposed, and serve immediately with flat leaf parsley scattered over the top, if liked.

4 soft corn tortillas
vegetable oil, for brushing
8 large eggs

**Ranchera sauce**
4 ripe tomatoes
½ onion, roughly chopped
1 garlic clove, roughly chopped
4 green chillies, roughly chopped
  (deseeded for a milder taste)
1 tablespoon vegetable oil
salt
chopped flat leaf parsley, to
  garnish (optional)

Serves **4**
Prep time **15 minutes**
Cooking time **15-20 minutes**

### Nutrient analysis per serving

| 1485 kJ | 355 kcal | energy |
|---|---|---|
| | 19 g | protein |
| | 26 g | carbohydrate |
| | 3 g | sugars |
| | 19 g | fat |
| | 4 g | saturates |
| | 2 g | fibre |
| | 275 mg | sodium |

AFFORDABILITY
1

# COURGETTE & MINT
## *Frittata*

2 teaspoons olive oil
1 onion, thinly sliced
2 courgettes, thinly sliced
6 eggs
2 tablespoons roughly chopped
  mint
salt and pepper

Serves **4**
Prep time **10 minutes**
Cooking time **25-35 minutes**

**1** Heat the oil in a heavy-based, nonstick 23 cm (9 inch) frying pan with a heatproof handle. Stir in the onion and cook over a low heat, stirring occasionally, for 10 minutes until softened, then stir in the courgettes and cook, stirring, for a further 2 minutes.

**2** Beat the eggs and mint together in a large bowl and season with salt and pepper. Stir in the cooked vegetables, then pour the mixture into the frying pan and quickly arrange the vegetables so that they are evenly dispersed. Cook over a low heat for 8-10 minutes or until all but the top of the frittata is set.

**3** Finish cooking under a preheated very hot grill, about 10 cm (4 inches) from the heat, until set but not coloured. Give the pan a shake to loosen the frittata or use a spatula, then transfer to a plate to cool. Cut into wedges and serve slightly warm or at room temperature.

## Healthy tip

EGGS ARE A RELATIVELY CHEAP SOURCE OF GOOD PROTEIN, AND ARE HIGH IN IRON AND VITAMINS A AND D. EGG YOLKS DO, HOWEVER, HAVE A HIGH CHOLESTEROL CONTENT, SO YOU SHOULD TRY TO LIMIT THE NUMBER YOU EAT EACH WEEK.

### Nutrient analysis per serving

| | | |
|---|---|---|
| 666 kJ | 160 kcal | energy |
| | 12 g | protein |
| | 5 g | carbohydrate |
| | 1 g | sugars |
| | 11 g | fat |
| | 3 g | saturates |
| | 0 g | fibre |
| | 117 mg | sodium |

# MEXICAN-STYLE
## *Scrambled* EGGS

1 Heat the oil in a large, heavy-based frying pan and gently sauté the onion until soft. Pour in the beaten eggs, chopped tomatoes and chillies. Season with salt.

2 Gently stir the egg mixture over the heat until set to your taste. Transfer to a warm dish and serve immediately.

1½ tablespoons vegetable oil
½ onion, finely chopped
8 large eggs, beaten
3 plum tomatoes, skinned, deseeded and finely chopped
2 green chillies, chopped (deseeded for a milder taste)
salt

Serves **4**
Prep time **10 minutes**
Cooking time **5-10 minutes**

### Good egg

This tried-and-tested formula means your soldiers won't be left languishing next to an overcooked egg. Put a few drops of vinegar into a pan of boiling water and carefully lower in your egg. Boil for 1 minute, then turn off the heat, cover the pan and leave the egg for a further 6 minutes. Remove and enjoy a perfectly cooked white and runny yolk.

### Nutrient analysis per serving

| 900 kJ | 217 kcal | energy |
|---|---|---|
| | 15 g | protein |
| | 3 g | carbohydrate |
| | 3 g | sugars |
| | 16 g | fat |
| | 4 g | saturates |
| | 1 g | fibre |
| | 164 mg | sodium |

# ROASTED TOFU
## WITH *Szechuan Relish*

1½ tablespoons olive oil
395 g (13¾ oz) silken firm tofu,
   cut into 2.5 cm (1 inch) cubes

**Szechuan relish**
250 g (8 oz) tomatoes, diced
100 g (3½ oz) cucumber, diced
1 red chilli, deseeded and sliced
2 tablespoons thinly sliced spring
   onions
½ garlic clove, crushed
½ teaspoon soft brown sugar
1 tablespoon lime juice
2 tablespoons chopped fresh
   coriander
½ teaspoon black pepper

Serves **4**
Prep time **10 minutes**
Cooking time **15-20 minutes**

1 Pour the olive oil into a large, foil-lined roasting tin and spread it with a brush. Arrange the tofu cubes evenly over the oil. Put the roasting tin on the top shelf of a preheated oven, 240°C (475°F), Gas Mark 9, and cook for 15-20 minutes or until the tofu is crisp and golden brown.

2 Meanwhile, make the Szechuan relish. Combine all the ingredients in a bowl and mix well. Set aside.

3 Put the roasted tofu cubes on a serving dish, spoon over the relish and serve.

AFFORDABILITY
1

### Nutrient analysis per serving

| 536 kJ | 129 kcal | energy |
|---|---|---|
| | 9 g | protein |
| | 3.9 g | carbohydrate |
| | 3.4 g | sugars |
| | 8.7 g | fat |
| | 1.2 g | saturates |
| | 0.9 g | fibre |
| | 12 mg | sodium |

AFFORDABILITY

**Nutrient analysis per serving**

| 166 kJ | 39 kcal | energy |
|---|---|---|
| | 1 g | protein |
| | 7 g | carbohydrate |
| | 1 g | sugars |
| | 1 g | fat |
| | 0 g | saturates |
| | 1 g | fibre |
| | 0.1 g | sodium |

# AUBERGINE &
# **POTATO** CAKES

1 Steam the aubergines and garlic for 6–8 minutes. Remove the garlic and peel, then mash them with the aubergines.

2 Steam the potatoes until cooked yet firm. Allow to cool, then grate coarsely and mix with the aubergines, onion, coriander, salt, cumin and paprika. Beat the egg white, fold it into the aubergine and potato mixture and leave for 5 minutes. Alternatively, to make shaping the cakes easier, put the mixture in the refrigerator for 5–10 minutes.

3 Oil your hands, take a portion of the mixture and form it into a 3 cm (1¼ inch) round. Heat the oil in a frying pan and fry the cakes until golden all over. Alternatively, grill for 3–5 minutes on each side until lightly browned, although they won't be as crisp. Drain on double kitchen paper and eat hot or at room temperature.

500 g (1 lb) aubergines, thickly sliced
4 garlic cloves, unpeeled
425 g (14 oz) potatoes, scrubbed and left whole
100 g (3½ oz) onion, grated
4 tablespoons finely chopped fresh coriander leaves
¾ teaspoon salt
½ teaspoon ground cumin, or to taste
pinch of paprika
1 egg white
groundnut oil, for oiling and frying

Serves **4**
Prep time **15 minutes, plus standing**
Cooking time **25-35 minutes**

# THREE **PEPPER** SALAD

AFFORDABILITY 1

250 g (8 oz) green peppers
250 g (8 oz) red peppers
250 g (8 oz) yellow peppers
1 small garlic clove
½ teaspoon salt
1 teaspoon apple cider vinegar
1¼ tablespoons lemon juice
1¼-1½ tablespoons extra virgin
   olive oil
¼ teaspoon ground cumin, or to
   taste
handful of parsley or fresh
   coriander leaves, finely chopped
pinch of black pepper (optional)

Serves **4**
Prep time **15 minutes**

1 Place the peppers on a heat diffuser (a metal circle that helps prevent pans from boiling over) or on a baking sheet over a medium gas flame and turn them for 3-5 minutes to char all over. Alternatively, preheat the grill to high, grill the peppers for 18 minutes or until charred on all sides. Leave to cool, then skin, core and deseed. Slice the flesh into thin strips.

2 Meanwhile, use a pestle and mortar to mash the garlic and salt. Incorporate the vinegar, lemon juice and oil and add to the peppers. Sprinkle with the cumin, parsley or coriander and pepper, if used. Toss, taste and adjust the seasonings if necessary, then serve.

**Nutrient analysis per serving**

| 420 kJ | 100 kcal | energy |
|---|---|---|
| | 3 g | protein |
| | 8 g | carbohydrate |
| | 8 g | sugars |
| | 6 g | fat |
| | 1 g | saturates |
| | 3 g | fibre |
| | 0.3 g | sodium |

# HARICOT
## BEAN SALAD

**1** Thoroughly rinse and drain the beans and them in a large saucepan with 450 ml (¾ pint) water. Bring slowly to the boil, skimming the surface as foam forms, then reduce the heat to low, cover and simmer for 20 minutes.

**2** Add the onions, ginger, tomatoes and oil and simmer, covered, for 15 minutes until the beans are tender.

**3** A few minutes before the end of the cooking time, mash the tomatoes against the side of the pan, then add the turmeric, vinegar, salt and pepper. Remove the pan from the heat, cover and leave until it reaches room temperature, then remove the ginger. Garnish with parsley sprigs, if liked, and serve.

200 g (7 oz) dried haricot beans, soaked for 6 hours
65 g (2½ oz) onions, grated
piece of fresh root ginger
125 g (4 oz) tomatoes, skinned, deseeded and sliced into chunks
½ tablespoon extra virgin olive oil
½ teaspoon turmeric
2 teaspoons apple cider vinegar
½ teaspoon salt
pinch of black pepper
flat leaf parsley sprigs, to garnish (optional)

Serves **2-4**
Prep time **20 minutes, plus soaking**
Cooking time **35 minutes**

**Nutrient analysis per serving**

| 1436 kJ | 338 kcal | energy |
|---|---|---|
| | 23 g | protein |
| | 57 g | carbohydrate |
| | 9 g | sugars |
| | 4 g | fat |
| | 1 g | saturates |
| | 25 g | fibre |
| | 0.8 g | sodium |

# BACHELOR OF
# BUDGET
## BAKES & PUDS

VICTORIA SPONGE

SCONES WITH WHIPPED CREAM

# CHOCOLATE CHIP COOKIES

125 g (4 oz) unsalted butter,
  softened, plus extra for greasing
50 g (2 oz) light soft brown sugar
1 egg, beaten
150 g (5 oz) self-raising flour
125 g (4 oz) plain dark chocolate,
  finely chopped

Makes **25**
Prep time **10 minutes**
Cooking time **15-20 minutes**

**1** Use the extra butter to lightly grease a baking sheet to prevent the cookies from sticking.

**2** Put the butter and sugar in a mixing bowl and beat together with a wooden spoon until light and fluffy. Beat in the egg, then sift in the flour. Add the chocolate pieces and mix thoroughly.

**3** Put 25 teaspoonfuls of the mixture slightly apart on the baking sheet and bake in a preheated oven, 180°C (350°F), Gas Mark 4, for 15-20 minutes until golden brown.

**4** Leave on the baking sheet for 1 minute, then transfer to a wire rack and leave to cool.

# PEANUT BUTTER COOKIES

1 Use the extra butter to lightly grease three large baking sheets to prevent the cookies from sticking.

2 Beat the butter and sugar together in a mixing bowl or a food processor until pale and creamy. Add the peanut butter, egg, flour and baking powder and stir together until combined. Stir in the peanuts.

3 Drop large teaspoonfuls of the mixture on to the baking sheets, leaving 5 cm (2 inch) gaps between each for them to spread during cooking. Flatten the mounds slightly and bake in a preheated oven, 190°C (375°F), Gas Mark 5, for 12 minutes until golden around the edges.

4 Leave to cool on the baking sheets for 2 minutes then transfer to a wire rack to cool completely.

125 g (4 oz) unsalted butter, at room temperature, plus extra for greasing
150 g (5 oz) soft brown sugar
125 g (4 oz) chunky peanut butter
1 egg, lightly beaten
150 g (5 oz) plain flour
½ teaspoon baking powder
125 g (4 oz) unsalted peanuts

Makes **32**
Prep time **10 minutes**
Cooking time **12 minutes**

AFFORDABILITY 1

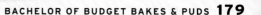

# FROSTED **CHOCOLATE** WHOOPIES

unsalted butter, for greasing
150 g (5 oz) self-raising flour
¼ teaspoon bicarbonate of soda
25 g (1 oz) cocoa powder
100 g (3½ oz) golden caster
 sugar
2 tablespoons vanilla sugar
1 egg
3 tablespoons vegetable oil
1 tablespoon milk
50 g (2 oz) plain or milk
 chocolate, chopped

**Filling**
100 g (3½ oz) cream cheese
2 tablespoons icing sugar, sifted
1 teaspoon finely grated orange
 rind
few drops of orange extract
 (optional)

Makes **12-14**
Prep time **20 minutes, plus
cooling**
Cooking time **15 minutes**

1 Use the butter to lightly grease a large baking sheet to prevent the whoopies from sticking.

2 Put the flour, bicarbonate of soda, cocoa powder and sugars in a bowl. Beat the egg with the vegetable oil and milk and add to the dry ingredients. Beat together to form a thick paste, adding a little more milk if the mixture feels crumbly.

3 Take teaspoonfuls of the mixture, flour your hands and roll the mixture into balls, about the size of a cherry. Space well apart on the baking sheet and flatten slightly.

4 Bake in a preheated oven, 200°C (400°F), Gas Mark 6, for 12 minutes until the mixture has spread and is pale golden. Transfer to a wire rack to cool.

5 Beat together the cream cheese, icing sugar, orange rind and extract and use it to sandwich the cakes together.

6 Put the chocolate in a small heatproof bowl over a pan of simmering water, making sure that the bottom of the bowl does not sit in the water. Melt the chocolate and spread it over the tops of the whoopies. (Alternatively, melt the chocolate in the microwave in 10-20 second bursts.)

AFFORDABILITY
2

# CHOCOLATE MOCHA BROWNIES

LIKE ALL THE BEST BROWNIE RECIPES, THIS VERSION IS BOTH GOOEY AND FUDGY.

1 Grease and line a shallow 27 x 18 cm (11 x 7 inch) rectangular tin or a 23 cm (9 inch) square tin.

2 Melt the plain chocolate with the butter in a heatproof bowl over a pan of simmering water, stirring frequently, until smooth. Stir in the coffee.

3 In a separate bowl beat together the eggs and sugar. Stir in the melted chocolate mixture, sift the flour and baking powder into the bowl and stir until they are combined.

4 Add the chopped milk chocolate and turn the mixture into the tin. Level the surface and bake in a preheated oven, 190°C (375°F), Gas Mark 5, for about 30 minutes or until a crust has formed but the mixture feels quite soft underneath. Leave to cool in the tin, then cut into squares.

175 g (6 oz) unsalted butter, plus extra for greasing
250 g (8 oz) plain dark chocolate, broken up
2 tablespoons instant coffee
3 eggs
225 g (7½ oz) light muscovado sugar
75 g (3 oz) self-raising flour
½ teaspoon baking powder
200 g (7 oz) milk chocolate, roughly chopped

Makes **15**
Prep time **15 minutes**
Cooking time **30 minutes**

## Freshen up your refrigerator

It doesn't take much more than a leftover take-away or a piece of ripe cheese to make your refrigerator smell like it should be condemned. Obviously, you need to remove the culinary culprits to stop the odours escalating, but a slice or two from a fresh lemon will help to freshen things up.

# JIM JAMS

125 g (4 oz) unsalted butter
125 g (4 oz) golden syrup
125 g (4 oz) light muscovado sugar
125 g (4 oz) oats
125 g (4 oz) self-raising wholemeal
  flour
25 g (1 oz) desiccated coconut

**To finish**
3 tablespoons strawberry jam
2 tablespoons desiccated coconut

Makes **9**
Prep time **10 minutes**
Cooking time **15-20 minutes**

1 Line an 18 cm (7 inch) shallow square cake tin with nonstick
  baking paper.

2 Heat butter, syrup and sugar gently in a saucepan until melted.
  Remove from the heat to stir in the oats, flour and coconut.

3 Press into an even layer in the tin and bake in a preheated
  oven, 180°C (350°F), Gas Mark 4, for 15 minutes until golden.

4 Leave to cool in the tin for 10 minutes, then mark into nine
  squares. Spread with the jam and sprinkle with the
coconut. Leave to cool completely.

5 Lift the paper out of the tin, cut the squares right through
  and peel off the paper. Store in an airtight tin for up to
three days.

AFFORDABILITY
2

# SCONES WITH
## *Whipped Cream*

1 Sift the flour, cream of tartar, bicarbonate of soda and salt into a mixing bowl and rub in the butter with your fingertips until the mixture resembles breadcrumbs. Stir in the sugar and add enough milk to mix to a soft dough.

2 Turn on to a floured surface, knead lightly and roll out to 1.5 cm (¾ inch) thick. Cut into 5 cm (2 inch) rounds with a biscuit cutter. Place on a floured baking sheet and brush with milk.

3 Bake in a preheated oven, 220°C (425°F), Gas Mark 7, for 10 minutes and transfer to a wire rack to cool. Serve with butter and jam or with whipped cream and jam.

250 g (8 oz) plain flour
1 teaspoon cream of tartar
½ teaspoon bicarbonate of soda
pinch of salt
50 g (2 oz) unsalted butter, chilled and diced
25 g (1 oz) caster sugar
about 125 ml (4 fl oz) milk, plus extra to glaze

**To serve**
butter or whipped cream
strawberry jam

Makes **10**
Prep time **10 minutes**
Cooking time **10 minutes**

AFFORDABILITY

1

# ROCK BUNS

AFFORDABILITY
2

THESE ARE QUICK AND EASY TO WHIZZ UP AND LOVELY WHEN EATEN FRESHLY BAKED. DON'T LET THEM HANG AROUND FOR TOO LONG THOUGH, OR THEY WILL LIVE UP TO THEIR INAPPROPRIATE NAME.

125 g (4 oz) unsalted butter,
  softened, plus extra for greasing
100 g (3½ oz) golden caster sugar
225 g (7½ oz) self-raising flour
1 teaspoon ground ginger
1 teaspoon ground cinnamon
1 egg, beaten
150 ml (¼ pint) milk
100 g (3½ oz) sultanas
75 g (3 oz) currants
50 g (2 oz) white sugar cubes

Makes **20**
Prep time **10 minutes**
Cooking time **15 minutes**

**1** Use the extra butter to lightly grease two baking sheets to prevent the buns from sticking.

**2** Cream together the butter and sugar until light and fluffy. Stir in the flour, spices, egg and milk and mix to a soft dough. Stir the dried fruits into the mixture.

**3** Place dessertspoonfuls of the mixture on the baking sheets, spacing them slightly apart.

**4** Put the sugar cubes in a polythene bag and lightly crush with a rolling pin. Scatter over the buns and bake in a preheated oven, 190°C (375°F), Gas Mark 5, for about 15 minutes or until risen and golden. Transfer to a wire rack to cool.

# BANANA **MUFFINS**

1 Line a deep muffin tin with 10 paper cases or lightly grease the cups.

2 Sift the flour, baking powder and cinnamon into a bowl. Stir in the nutmeg, almonds and sugar.

3 Lightly mash the bananas and mix in the eggs, oil, milk and honey to make a sloppy paste. Work the banana mixture into the dry ingredients, first using a fork and then folding in with a tablespoon.

4 Spoon the muffin batter into the paper cases or greased cups and bake in a preheated oven, 190°C (375°F), Gas Mark 5, for 25 minutes (check after 20 minutes) or until well risen. When they are done a skewer inserted in the centre should come out clean. Leave for 5 minutes, then transfer to a wire rack to cool.

200 g (7 oz) plain white organic flour
3 teaspoons baking powder
1½ teaspoons ground cinnamon
grated nutmeg
50 g (2 oz) ground almonds
50 g (2 oz) soft brown sugar
2 large ripe bananas, about 350 g (11½ oz) unpeeled or 250 g (8 oz) peeled
2 eggs
2 tablespoons sunflower oil
125 ml (4 fl oz) skimmed milk
3 tablespoons clear honey

Makes **10**
Prep time **20 minutes**
Cooking time **20-25 minutes**

## Keep your oven clean

Ovens are a serious pain to clean, so anything you can do to avoid this loathsome task is a benefit. Line grill pans and oven trays with a layer of kitchen foil, tucking it down so that the sides of the trays are protected too. When they get really dirty, you can swap the foil and the trays will be pristine.

AFFORDABILITY 2

# BLUEBERRY & VANILLA MUFFINS

AFFORDABILITY
2

150 g (5 oz) ground almonds
150 g (5 oz) golden caster sugar
50 g (2 oz) self-raising flour
175 g (6 oz) unsalted butter, melted
4 egg whites
1 teaspoon vanilla extract
150 g (5 oz) blueberries

Makes **10**
Prep time **5 minutes**
Cooking time **15 minutes**

1 Line 10 sections of a muffin tray with paper cases or grease the sections.

2 Mix together the ground almonds, sugar, flour and butter. Add the egg whites and vanilla extract and combine until the mixture is a smooth paste.

3 Spoon into the cases and scatter with the blueberries. Bake in a preheated oven, 220°C (425°F), Gas Mark 7, for 15 minutes until just firm in the centre. Leave for 5 minutes, then transfer the muffins to a wire rack to cool.

AFFORDABILITY 1

# TRIPLE
## CHOCOLATE
## MUFFINS

50 g (2 oz) plain chocolate chips
50 g (2 oz) unsalted butter
2 eggs
75 g (3 oz) caster sugar
75 g (3 oz) self-raising flour
25 g (1 oz) cocoa powder
25 g (1 oz) white chocolate chips

Makes **10**
Prep time **12 minutes**
Cooking time **12 minutes**

**1** Line 10 sections of a muffin tray with paper cases or grease the sections.

**2** Carefully melt the plain chocolate chips with the butter in a small, heavy-based pan set over a low heat.

**3** Beat together the eggs, sugar, flour and cocoa powder in a large bowl. With a metal spatula, fold in the melted chocolate mixture and the white chocolate chips.

**4** Spoon the mixture into the paper cases and bake in a preheated oven, 180°C (350°F), Gas Mark 4, for 12 minutes or until risen and firm to the touch. Transfer the muffins to a wire rack to cool slightly before eating.

# VICTORIA SPONGE

**1** Use the extra butter to lightly grease two 18 cm (7 inch) sandwich tins and line the bases with a circle of greaseproof paper or nonstick baking paper.

**2** Put the butter and sugar in a mixing bowl and beat together with a wooden spoon until pale and creamy. Gradually beat in the eggs and vanilla extract, a little at a time, adding 1 tablespoon of flour with each addition to help prevent the mixture from curdling.

**3** Sift the remaining flour and baking powder into the bowl and fold gently into the creamed mixture.

**4** Spoon the mixture into the cake tins and spread the tops level. Bake in a preheated oven, 180°C (350°F), Gas Mark 4, for about 20 minutes or until the cake will spring back when lightly pressed with a fingertip. Leave to cool for 5 minutes, then loosen and turn the cakes out on to a wire rack, peel off the lining paper and leave to cool.

**5** Put one of the cakes, top downwards, on a serving plate and spread with the jam. Top with the second cake and dust the top with sifted icing sugar.

175 g (6 oz) unsalted butter, at room temperature, plus extra for greasing
175 g (6 oz) caster sugar
3 eggs
1 teaspoon vanilla extract
175 g (6 oz) self-raising flour
1 teaspoon baking powder
3 tablespoons strawberry jam
icing sugar, for dusting

Serves **8**
Prep time **15 minutes**
Cooking time **20-25 minutes**

AFFORDABILITY
**1**

# LEMON *Drizzle* CAKE

ASK ANYONE TO LIST THEIR FAVOURITE CAKES, AND THIS WILL ALMOST CERTAINLY BE ONE OF THEM.

225 g (7½ oz) unsalted butter, softened, plus extra for greasing
225 g (7½ oz) caster sugar
finely grated rind of 3 lemons
4 eggs, beaten
250 g (8 oz) self-raising flour
1 teaspoon baking powder
75 g (3 oz) ground almonds
100 ml (3½ fl oz) lemon juice
100 g (3½ oz) granulated sugar

Serves **8-10**
Prep time **20 minutes**
Cooking time **50-60 minutes**

1 Grease and line the base and sides of a 20 cm (8 inch) round cake tin or an 18 cm (7 inch) square tin. Lightly grease the paper.

2 Cream together the butter, caster sugar and lemon rind until light and fluffy. Beat in the eggs, a little at a time, beating well between each addition. Add a little of the flour if the mixture starts to curdle.

3 Sift the flour and baking powder into the bowl, add the ground almonds and 2 tablespoons lemon juice and gently fold in using a large metal spoon.

4 Turn the mixture into the tin and level the surface. Bake in a preheated oven, 180°C (350°F), Gas Mark 4, for about 45 minutes or until just firm and a skewer inserted into the centre comes out clean.

5 Meanwhile, mix together the remaining lemon juice with the granulated sugar. Transfer the cake to a wire rack. Give the lemon mixture a good stir and spoon it over the cake. As the cake cools the syrup will sink into the cake, leaving a sugary crust.

# CARROT CAKE

**1** Lightly grease and line the base and sides of a 20 cm (8 inch) round cake tin.

**2** Put the butter, sugar, eggs, orange rind, flour, baking powder, ground nuts and ginger together in a bowl and beat until smooth and creamy.

**3** Stir in the carrots and raisins until evenly combined and turn the mixture into the tin. Level the surface and bake in a preheated oven, 180°C (350°F), Gas Mark 4, for about 1 hour or until just firm and a skewer inserted into the centre comes out clean. Transfer to a wire rack to cool.

**4** Make the cream cheese frosting. Put the cream cheese in a bowl and beat until it is softened and smooth. Add 1 teaspoon lemon juice and the icing sugar and beat until smooth, adding a little more juice if the mixture is too firm.

**5** Use a palette knife to spread the top and sides of the cake with the frosting. Decorate with toasted hazelnuts.

225 g (7½ oz) unsalted butter, softened, plus extra for greasing
225 g (7½ oz) light muscovado sugar
4 eggs
grated rind of 1 orange
175 g (6 oz) self-raising flour, sifted
1 teaspoon baking powder, sifted
75 g (3 oz) ground hazelnuts
65 g (2½ oz) stem ginger, chopped
300 g (10 oz) carrots, finely grated
75 g (3 oz) raisins
toasted hazelnuts, roughly chopped, to decorate

**Cream cheese frosting**
200 g (7 oz) full-fat cream cheese
1-2 teaspoons lime or lemon juice
75 g (3 oz) icing sugar, sifted

Serves **10-12**
Prep time **30 minutes**
Cooking time **1 hour**

# CHOCOLATE FUDGE CUPCAKES

40 g (1½ oz) cocoa powder
100 ml (3½ fl oz) boiling water
50 g (2 oz) lightly salted butter,
  softened
125 g (4 oz) light muscovado sugar
1 egg
100 g (3½ oz) self-raising flour
150 g (5 oz) raspberries, to
  decorate

**Frosting**
75 g (3 oz) plain dark chocolate,
  chopped
1 tablespoon milk
25 g (1 oz) lightly salted butter
25 g (1 oz) icing sugar, plus extra
  for dusting

Makes **16**
Prep time **25 minutes, plus
cooling**
Cooking time **12 minutes**

1 Put 16 mini silicone ovenproof muffin cases onto a baking sheet.

2 Whisk the cocoa powder with the boiling water in a bowl. Leave to cool.

3 Beat together the butter and muscovado sugar in a separate bowl until pale and creamy. Gradually beat in the egg. Sift in the flour and stir in the cocoa mixture.

4 Spoon the batter into the cases and bake in a preheated oven, 180°C (350°F), Gas Mark 4, for 8-10 minutes until risen and just firm to the touch. Leave in the cases for 2 minutes, then transfer to a wire rack to cool.

5 Put the chocolate, milk and butter in a saucepan and heat gently until melted and a smooth sauce forms. Remove from the heat. Sift the icing sugar into the chocolate mixture and stir well. Use a palette knife to spread the frosting over the cakes. Leave to cool completely. Scatter with the raspberries and serve lightly dusted with icing sugar.

AFFORDABILITY
1

# MALTY FRUIT CAKE

THIS IS AN EASY AND WHOLESOME CAKE, PERFECT FOR WHEN YOU WANT TO MAKE SOMETHING QUICKLY FOR TEA OR SNACKS.

**1** Grease and line the base and sides of a 500 g (1 lb) loaf tin, making the paper come at least 1 cm (½ inch) above the rim of the tin. Grease the paper.

**2** Mix together the fruit, sugar, malt extract, bran, spices and milk in a bowl and leave to stand for 20 minutes.

**3** Stir in the flour, turn the mixture into the tin and bake in a preheated oven, 160°C (325°F), Gas Mark 3, for about 50 minutes or until a skewer inserted into the centre comes out clean. Transfer to a wire rack to cool.

unsalted butter, for greasing
175 g (6 oz) luxury mixed dried fruit
125 g (4 oz) dark muscovado sugar
3 tablespoons malt extract
100 g (3½ oz) shredded bran or bran-flake cereal
1 teaspoon ground cinnamon
½ teaspoon grated nutmeg
300 ml (½ pint) milk
150 g (5 oz) self-raising flour

Serves **8**
Prep time **10 minutes, plus soaking**
Cooking time **50 minutes**

# SWEET
# CHEATS

◇◇◇◇◇◇◇◇◇◇◇◇◇◇◇◇◇◇◇◇◇◇◇◇◇◇◇◇◇◇◇◇◇◇◇◇◇◇◇◇◇◇◇◇◇◇◇◇◇◇◇

There's nothing like a lovingly prepared pudding for a show-stopping dinner party finale, but if you've been sweating over a hot stove all day long just to get a main course on the table, you might have left yourself a bit short of time to rustle up a pudding. If so, don't panic – help is at hand. With a few basic ingredients you can create a happy ending for your meal that will wow your mates but won't send you over the culinary edge.

## ICE CREAM SURPRISE

Ice cream might sound like a cop-out for pudding, but not if you jazz it up with a few surprises. Buy a tub of any ordinary, plain vanilla ice cream and a selection of small sweets. Let the ice cream soften slightly for a minute or two, then mix in the sweets and pop the ice cream back in the freezer. If you have a sudden last-minute burst of creativity, you could serve it with Glossy Chocolate Sauce (see page 236) spooned over the top.

## HOT CHOCOLATE

Not strictly speaking a dess but hot chocolate with cre and mini marshmallow always a t

## FEELING FRUITY

This does, it must be said, involve a tiny bit of cooking, but it's nothing more complicated than turning on the oven – honestly. Turn on the oven to about 200°C (400°F), Gas Mark 6, and, while you're waiting for it to reach the required temperature, cut in half as many peaches as you have guests and take out the stones. Put the peaches on a baking tray and drizzle over a little orange juice, fruit liqueur or red wine, then sprinkle generously with brown sugar. Bake the peaches for about 20 minutes and serve with a dollop of ice cream or double cream.

## ETON MESS

This dessert is so easy to make. Break up some mini shop-bought meringue nests into a large mixing bowl (try to get a mixture of chunky and fine pieces), add some chopped strawberries and raspberries and a carton of extra thick double cream. Mix carefully so that the berries don't completely disintegrate, then spoon the mixture into your best serving dishes and serve.

## TRICK TRIFLE

Who doesn't like sponge, fruit and custard piled high into a bowl? Select your biggest glasses and line the bases with pieces of shop-bought sponge cake. Put pieces of chopped tinned fruit into the glasses, spooning a bit of the juice over as well. Then pour over some ready-made custard and sprinkle with chocolate shavings or hundreds and thousands. Put the trifles in the refrigerator until you're ready to eat them.

AFFORDABILITY
1

# PANCAKE STACK
## WITH MAPLE SYRUP

1 egg
75 g (3 oz) plain flour, sifted
100 ml (3½ fl oz) milk
2½ tablespoons vegetable oil
1 tablespoon caster sugar
maple syrup, for drizzling
8 scoops of vanilla ice cream, to
   serve

Serves **4**
Prep time **10 minutes**
Cooking time **6 minutes**

**1** Make the batter. Put the egg, flour, milk, oil and sugar in a blender or food processor and whizz until smooth and creamy.

**2** Heat a frying pan over a medium heat and pour a ladleful of the batter into each corner to make four pancakes. After about 1 minute the tops of the pancakes will start to set and air bubbles will rise to the top and burst. Use a spatula to turn the pancakes over and cook on the other side for 1 minute.

**3** Repeat twice more until you have used all the batter, making 12 small pancakes in all. Bring to the table as a stack, drizzled with maple syrup. Serve three pancakes to each person with two scoops of ice cream.

# VANILLA & BANANA
# PANCAKES

1 Mash the bananas with the vanilla extract in a bowl to make a smooth purée. Sift the flour and baking powder into a separate bowl and stir in the sugar.

2 Beat the egg, milk and melted butter together in another bowl and beat into the dry ingredients until smooth. Stir in the banana purée.

3 Heat a little oil in a large frying pan or griddle pan over a medium heat. Using a large metal spoon, drop four spoonfuls of the batter, well spaced apart, in the pan and cook for 2 minutes or until bubbles form on the surfaces and the undersides are golden brown. Use a spatula to turn the pancakes over and cook on the other side for 1-2 minutes. Remove from the pan, wrap in a tea towel and keep warm while you cook the remaining batter in the same way.

4 Transfer the pancakes to a serving plate and serve with maple syrup.

2 ripe bananas
1 teaspoon vanilla extract
150 g (5 oz) self-raising flour
1 teaspoon baking powder
1 tablespoon caster sugar
1 egg
75 ml (3 fl oz) milk
1 tablespoon unsalted butter, melted
sunflower oil, for frying
maple syrup, to serve

Serves **4**
Prep time **15 minutes**
Cooking time **15 minutes**

# BUTTERMILK **PANCAKES** WITH **BLUEBERRY** SAUCE

250 g (8 oz) fresh blueberries
2 tablespoons clear honey
dash of lemon juice
15 g (½ oz) unsalted butter
150 g (5 oz) self-raising flour
1 teaspoon bicarbonate of soda
40 g (1½ oz) caster sugar
1 egg, beaten
350 ml (12 fl oz) buttermilk
Greek yogurt or crème fraîche, to
  serve
icing sugar, for dusting

Serves **4-6**
Prep time **10 minutes**
Cooking time **16 minutes**

1 Put the berries, honey and a dash of lemon juice in a small saucepan and warm gently for about 3 minutes until the berries release their juices. Keep warm.

2 Melt the butter in a small pan. Sift the flour and bicarbonate of soda together into a bowl and stir in the sugar. Beat the egg and buttermilk together and gradually whisk into the dry ingredients with the melted butter to make a smooth batter.

3 Heat a nonstick frying pan until hot and drop in large spoonfuls of batter. Cook for 3 minutes, until bubbles appear on the surface. Use a spatula to turn the pancakes over and cook for a further minute. Keep warm while you cook the remainder.

4 Serve the pancakes topped with the blueberry sauce and some Greek yogurt or crème fraîche. Dust with icing sugar before serving.

AFFORDABILITY
2

# Toffee Apple
# BAKE

**1** Toss the apples in a shallow ovenproof dish with 1 tablespoonful of the flour and the muscovado sugar.

**2** Mix the remaining flour with the caster sugar and spice in a bowl. Add the egg, yogurt and butter and stir lightly until only just combined.

**3** Spoon the mixture over the apples and bake in a preheated oven, 220°C (425°F), Gas Mark 7, for 15-20 minutes until just firm and golden. Serve warm.

3 dessert apples, cored and thickly sliced
100 g (3½ oz) self-raising flour, plus 1 tablespoon extra
125 g (4 oz) light muscovado sugar
50 g (2 oz) caster sugar
½ teaspoon ground mixed spice
1 egg
100 ml (3½ fl oz) natural yogurt
50 g (2 oz) unsalted butter, melted

Serves **4**
Prep time **10 minutes**
Cooking time **15-20 minutes**

AFFORDABILITY
2

## Milking it

Fact: student houses always run out of milk. Fact: you can freeze milk. So if you don't want to develop the taste for black tea and coffee, keep a sneaky pint of milk tucked away at the back of the freezer, and you won't have to choose between curdled milk or an early-morning trip to the shops.

# *Sticky* TOFFEE
# PUDDINGS

4 tablespoons double cream, plus extra to serve

50 g (2 oz) butter, separated into quarters

4 tablespoons soft light brown sugar

**Sponge**

25 g (1 oz) walnuts, finely chopped

125 g (4 oz) unsalted butter, softened

125 g (4 oz) soft light brown sugar

2 eggs

75 g (3 oz) self-raising flour

Serves **4**

Prep time **5 minutes**

Cooking time **20-25 minutes**

**1** Divide the cream, butter and sugar evenly into four ramekins or timbales.

**2** Make the sponge. Put the walnuts, butter, sugar, eggs and flour in a food processor and process until smooth. Spoon the batter over the toffee mixture and smooth flat.

**3** Bake in a preheated oven, 190°C (375°F), Gas Mark 5, for 20-25 minutes until risen and lightly golden. Turn out and serve with extra cream, lightly whipped.

# CHOCOLATE
## BREAD & BUTTER
### *Pudding*

**1** Lightly grease a 1.2 litre (2 pint) shallow, round, ovenproof pie dish.

**2** Slice the croissants thickly and spread the butter over one side of each cut face. Stand the croissant slices upright and close together in the dish to completely fill it.

**3** Mix together the sugar and spice and spoon over the croissants and between the gaps. Stand the dish in a large roasting tin.

**4** Beat together the milk, eggs and vanilla extract and strain into the dish. Leave to stand for 15 minutes.

**5** Pour hot water from the tap into the roasting tin to come halfway up the sides of the pie dish and bake in a preheated oven, 180°C (350°F), Gas Mark 4, for about 25 minutes until the pudding is golden and the custard just set.

**6** Lift the dish out of the roasting tin, dust with sifted icing sugar and serve the pudding warm with a little pouring cream.

50 g (2 oz) unsalted butter, plus
  extra for greasing
4 chocolate croissants
50 g (2 oz) caster sugar
¼ teaspoon ground mixed spice
300 ml (½ pint) milk
4 eggs
1 teaspoon vanilla extract
icing sugar, for dusting
pouring cream, to serve

Serves **4**
Prep time **20 minutes, plus standing**
Cooking time **25 minutes**

# LEMON
## *Puddle*
# PUDDING

AFFORDABILITY **1**

75 g (3 oz) unsalted butter, at
  room temperature, plus extra for
  greasing
150 g (5 oz) caster sugar
grated rind of 2 lemons
3 eggs, separated
50 g (2 oz) self-raising flour, sifted
300 ml (½ pint) milk
4 tablespoons lemon juice
icing sugar, for dusting (optional)

Serves **4**
Prep time **20 minutes**
Cooking time **25-30 minutes**

**1** Lightly grease a 1.2 litre (2 pint) pie dish and stand the dish in a roasting tin.

**2** Put the butter in a mixing bowl with the sugar and lemon rind. Whisk the egg whites in a separate bowl until they are softly peaking. Using the still dirty whisk, beat the butter, sugar and lemon rind until light and fluffy, then mix in the flour and egg yolks.

**3** Combine the milk and lemon juice gradually until only just mixed. (The mixture may appear to separate slightly but this will disappear during baking.) Add to the batter.

**4** Fold in the egg whites, then gently pour the mixture into the pie dish. Pour hot water from the tap into the roasting tin to come halfway up the sides of the dish and bake in a preheated oven, 190°C (375°F), Gas Mark 5, for about 25 minutes until slightly risen, golden brown and the top has begun to crack. Insert a knife into the centre: the top two-thirds should be soufflé-like and the bottom third a saucy, custard-like layer. If it's very soft in the centre, cook for an extra 5 minutes.

**5** Dust the top with a little sifted icing sugar, if liked, then serve immediately spooned into shallow bowls. Don't leave the dessert to stand or the topping will absorb the sauce.

# BAKED PEAR
## WITH ALMOND
## CRUMBLE

75 g (3 oz) wholemeal flour
65 g (2½ oz) ground almonds
75 g (3 oz) soft light brown sugar
65 g (2½ oz) unsalted butter,
 diced
4 pears, quartered, cored and
 sliced lengthways
juice of 1 lime
2 tablespoons flaked almonds
150 ml (¼ pint) crème fraîche, to
 serve (optional)

Serves **4**
Prep time **10 minutes**
Cooking time **20 minutes**

1 Mix together the flour, ground almonds and sugar in a
 large bowl. Add the butter and rub in with your
fingertips until the mixture resembles fine breadcrumbs.

2 Arrange the pear slices in four tall, ovenproof
 ramekins and drizzle with the lime juice. Cover the
pears with the crumble mixture and sprinkle over the
flaked almonds.

3 Bake in a preheated oven, 220°C (425°F), Gas Mark 7,
 for 20 minutes. Serve warm, topped with crème
fraîche, if liked.

AFFORDABILITY 2

# RICE Pudding

AFFORDABILITY
1

1 Rinse the rice briefly under the cold tap to remove any impurities, drain and soak for 15 minutes in boiling water. Rinse well and drain.

2 Put the milk, sugar, salt, vanilla pod, cinnamon stick and lime and orange rind in a heavy-based saucepan and bring slowly to the boil, stirring constantly. Remove from the heat and leave to infuse for 10 minutes. Remove the lime and orange rind and discard. Remove the vanilla pod, slit it open and scrape out the seeds into the milk.

3 Add the rice to the milk and bring to the boil over a medium heat. Reduce the heat, cover and gently simmer until the rice is cooked and the mixture thickens. Stir in the raisins. You may need some more cold milk to adjust the consistency: the rice must not be dry.

4 Remove from the heat and leave to cool, then transfer the pudding to a serving dish, cover and refrigerate until required. Serve cold, dusted with cinnamon to decorate.

200 g (7 oz) long grain white rice
1.5 litres (2½ pints) semi-skimmed milk
100 g (3½ oz) caster sugar
pinch of salt
1 vanilla pod
1 cinnamon stick, broken into 2-3 pieces
thinly pared rind of 1 lime
thinly pared rind of 1 orange
50 g (2 oz) raisins
ground cinnamon, for dusting

Serves **6-8**
Prep time **10 minutes, plus soaking and infusing**
Cooking time **15 minutes**

# **CHOCOLATE** RISOTTO

600 ml (1 pint) milk
25 g (1 oz) sugar
50 g (2 oz) butter
125 g (4 oz) arborio or carnaroli
   rice
50 g (2 oz) hazelnuts, toasted and
   chopped
50 g (2 oz) sultanas
125 g (4 oz) good-quality plain
   dark chocolate, grated
splash of brandy (optional)
grated chocolate, to decorate

Serves **4**
Prep time **5 minutes**
Cooking time **20 minutes**

1 Put the milk and sugar into a saucepan and heat to simmering point.

2 Melt the butter in a heavy-based saucepan, add the rice and stir well to coat the grains.

3 Add a ladleful of hot milk to the rice and stir well. When the rice has absorbed the milk, add another ladleful. Continue to add the milk in stages and stir until it is all absorbed. The rice should be just tender with a creamy sauce.

4 Add the hazelnuts, sultanas and grated chocolate and mix quickly. Serve decorated with a little grated chocolate. Try not to over-mix the chocolate because the marbled effect looks good. For a special treat, add a splash of brandy just before decorating and serving the risotto.

AFFORDABILITY
3

# CHOCOLATE & RASPBERRY *Pudding*

olive oil spray, for oiling
175 g (6 oz) fresh raspberries
125 g (4 oz) self-raising flour
40 g (1½ oz) cocoa powder
100 g (3½ oz) caster sugar
250 ml (8 fl oz) milk
75 g (3 oz) unsalted butter, melted
2 eggs, beaten

**Topping**
75 g (3 oz) caster sugar
75 g (3 oz) soft light brown sugar
2 tablespoons cocoa powder
350 ml (12 fl oz) boiling water
icing sugar, for dusting

Serves **6**
Prep time **15 minutes, plus resting**
Cooking time **40-45 minutes**

**1** Spray a 1 litre (1¾ pint) baking dish lightly with spray olive oil to prevent the pudding from sticking.

**2** Scatter a layer of raspberries evenly over the base of the dish.

**3** Sift the flour and cocoa powder into a bowl and stir in the caster sugar. Make a well in the centre and whisk in the milk, melted butter and eggs to form a smooth batter (the batter should be quite runny). Pour the mixture into the dish, covering the raspberries.

**4** Make the topping. Combine the sugars and cocoa powder and sprinkle over the top of the chocolate mixture. Carefully pour the boiling water over the top of the mixture as evenly as possible.

**5** Bake in a preheated oven, 180°C (350°F), Gas Mark 4, for 40-45 minutes until the pudding is firm to the touch and some 'bubbles' of sauce appear on the top. Rest for 5 minutes, then dust with icing sugar and serve.

# Sticky Rice WITH MANGO

250 g (8 oz) white sticky rice
100 ml (3½ fl oz) coconut milk
2 tablespoons palm or coconut
  sugar
½ teaspoon salt (optional)
4 ripe mangoes

Serves **4**
Prep time **20 minutes, plus
soaking and resting**
Cooking time **30-35 minutes**

**1** Soak the rice in a bowl of water for at least 3 hours. Drain the rice and transfer it to a steamer basket lined with a double thickness of muslin. Spread the rice in the steamer.

**2** Bring the water to a rolling boil. Taking care not to burn your hand, set the steamer basket over the water, reduce the heat, cover and steam for 20-25 minutes or until the rice swells and is glistening and tender. Check and replenish the water every 10 minutes or so.

**3** Mix the coconut milk and sugar with 50 ml (2 fl oz) water in a small saucepan and stir over a low heat until the sugar has dissolved.

**4** As soon as the rice is cooked, spoon it into a bowl, mix it with the coconut milk mixture, cover and leave to rest for 10 minutes.

**5** Peel the mangoes and slice off the outside cheeks of each, removing as much flesh as you can in large pieces. (Avoid cutting very close to the stone where the flesh is fibrous.) Discard the stone. Slice each piece of mango into 4-5 pieces lengthways, arrange on a serving plate and spoon a portion of sticky rice and coconut milk next to them.

AFFORDABILITY **1**

# CARAMELIZED ORANGE & PINEAPPLE

1 Use a small, sharp knife to remove the rind from two of the oranges and slice it into very fine strips. Put the rind in a saucepan of boiling water and simmer for 2 minutes. Remove and drain well.

2 Put the sugar in a heavy-based saucepan, add 125 ml (4 fl oz) water and heat gently, swishing the pan constantly until the sugar is dissolved. Increase the heat and boil the syrup until it turns golden brown. Take care not to overcook the caramel; if it gets too dark, carefully add 2 tablespoons of water. Stand back when you add the water because the caramel will spit. Set aside when ready.

3 To peel the oranges, cut a slice off the top and bottom of each one, then place the orange on one of these cut sides and take a knife around the side of the orange, cutting away the skin and pith. Cut across the orange into about 6-7 slices.

4 To prepare the pineapple, top and tail it and slice away the skin from top to bottom. Make sure that you remove the 'eyes' close to the skin. Cut the pineapple into quarters and remove the core. Cut into slices.

5 Make alternate layers of orange and pineapple in a heatproof dish. Sprinkle with the orange rind, pour over the caramel and leave to stand until required.

4 oranges
175 g (6 oz) sugar
1 small pineapple

Serves **4**
Prep time **10 minutes**
Cooking time **10 minutes**

AFFORDABILITY
1

# BAKED **PEACHES**
# WITH ALMONDS
# & HONEY

50 g (2 oz) unsalted butter, plus
    extra for greasing
4 large ripe peaches, halved and
    stoned
50 g (2 oz) flaked almonds
4 tablespoons clear honey
a little ground cinnamon
crème fraîche, to serve

Serves **4**
Prep time **5 minutes**
Cooking time **15 minutes**

**1** Butter a shallow baking dish that is large enough to hold 8 peach halves.

**2** Put the peaches in the baking dish, skin side down, and dot with butter. Sprinkle with the almonds, drizzle with the honey and dust with cinnamon.

**3** Bake the peaches at the top of a preheated oven, 200°C (400°F), Gas Mark 6, for 10–15 minutes, until there is a little colour into the peaches and the almonds have browned slightly.

**4** Serve the peaches with the juices drizzled over and topped with a spoonful of crème fraîche.

AFFORDABILITY

# PANETTONE
# **PUDDING**

1 Use the butter to grease the bottom and sides of a 1.2 litre (2 pint) ovenproof dish.

2 Spread the panettone slices with apricot jam and cut them into triangles or rectangles. Arrange them in the dish in overlapping layers.

3 Put the milk and cream into a saucepan and bring gently to the boil.

4 Whisk together the eggs, egg yolk and sugar in a bowl until creamy and fluffy. Continue whisking and slowly add the hot milk and cream. When it is all combined, carefully pour it over the panettone slices, making sure they are completely covered by the custard mixture. Sprinkle with a little extra sugar to make a crunchy crust.

5 Stand the panettone pudding in a roasting tin and half-fill it with boiling water. Bake in a preheated oven, 180°C (350°F), Gas Mark 4, for 25 minutes or until the custard is set.

50 g (2 oz) butter
5 slices of panettone
apricot jam, for spreading
250 ml (8 fl oz) milk
250 ml (8 fl oz) double cream
2 eggs
1 egg yolk
50 g (2 oz) brown sugar, plus
  extra for the crust

Serves **4**
Prep time **5 minutes**
Cooking time **25 minutes**

# DEEP DISH PUFF APPLE PIE

1 kg (2 lb) or about 5 cooking
  apples, quartered, cored, peeled
  and thickly sliced
100 g (3½ oz) caster sugar, plus
  extra for sprinkling
grated rind of 1 small orange
½ teaspoon ground mixed spice
  or ground cinnamon
3 whole cloves
400 g (13 oz) chilled puff pastry
beaten egg, to glaze
crème fraîche or double cream, to
  serve

Serves **6**
Prep time **40 minutes**
Cooking time **20-25 minutes**

**1** Fill a 1.2 litre (2 pint) pie dish with the apple slices. Mix the sugar with the orange rind, mixed spice or cinnamon and cloves and sprinkle over the apples.

**2** Roll out the pastry on a lightly floured surface until it is a little larger than the top of the dish. Cut two long strips from the edges, about 1 cm (½ inch) wide. Brush the dish rim with a little beaten egg, press the strips on top, then brush these with egg. Lift the remaining pastry over the dish and press the edges together well.

**3** Trim off the excess pastry, knock up the edges with a small knife, then flute the edges by pinching the layers of pastry between your fingers and thumb. Re-roll the trimmings and cut out small heart shapes or circles with a small biscuit cutter. Brush the top of the pie with beaten egg, add the pastry shapes and brush these with egg. Sprinkle with a little extra sugar.

**4** Bake in a preheated oven, 200°C (400°F), Gas Mark 6, for 20-25 minutes until the pastry is well risen and golden. Serve warm with spoonfuls of crème fraîche or extra-thick cream.

AFFORDABILITY
**1**

### Stick the knife in

It's better to have one sharp knife than a whole block of blunt ones. A good all-round chopping knife is essential for quick food preparation.

# PUMPKIN
# PIE

1 Lightly grease a 23 cm (9 inch) x 2.5 cm (1 inch) deep enamel pie dish. Cut the pumpkin or butternut squash into cubes and cook in a covered steamer for 15-20 minutes until tender. Cool, then purée in a liquidizer or food processor.

2 Whisk the eggs, sugar, flour and spices together in a bowl until just mixed. Add the pumpkin purée and whisk together. Gradually mix in the milk and set aside.

3 Roll out three-quarters of the pastry on a lightly floured surface until it is large enough to line the pie dish. Lift the pastry over the rolling pin and press it over the base and sides of the dish. Trim off the excess around the rim and add the trimmings to the reserved pastry. Roll this out thinly and cut leaves, then mark veins. Brush the rim of the pastry in the dish, then press on the leaves, reserving a few. Stand the dish on a baking sheet.

4 Pour the pumpkin filling into the dish, add a few leaves, if liked, on top of the filling and brush these and the dish edges lightly with milk. Bake in a preheated oven, 190°C (375°F), Gas Mark 5, for 45-55 minutes until the filling is set and the pastry is cooked through. Cover with kitchen foil after 20 minutes to stop the pastry edge from over-browning.

5 Serve dusted with a little icing sugar and with whipped cream sprinkled with a little extra ground spice, if liked.

unsalted butter, for greasing
500 g (1 lb) pumpkin or butternut squash, weighed after deseeding and peeling
3 eggs
100 g (3½ oz) light muscovado sugar
2 tablespoons plain flour
½ teaspoon ground cinnamon
½ teaspoon ground ginger
¼ teaspoon grated nutmeg
200 ml (7 fl oz) milk, plus extra for glazing
450 g (14½ oz) chilled sweet shortcrust pastry
flour, for dusting

**To serve**
icing sugar
whipped cream
ground spice

Serves **6**
Prep time **30 minutes**
Cooking time **1-1¼ hours**

# BANOFFEE PIE

200 g (7 oz) unsalted butter, plus extra for greasing
2 tablespoons golden syrup
250 g (8 oz) digestive biscuits, crushed
100 g (3½ oz) dark muscovado sugar
400 g (13 oz) can full-fat condensed milk
300 ml (½ pint) double cream
3 small ripe bananas
4 tablespoons lemon juice
grated plain dark chocolate, to decorate

Serves **6**
Prep time **35 minutes, plus chilling and cooling**
Cooking time **8 minutes**

1 Lightly grease a 20 cm (8 inch) springform cake tin with some of the unsalted butter.

2 Melt half the butter and the syrup in a saucepan, add the biscuit crumbs and mix well. Tip into the cake tin press evenly over the base and up the sides almost to the top. Chill.

3 Heat the remaining butter and the sugar in a nonstick frying pan until the butter has melted and the sugar has dissolved. Add the condensed milk and cook over a medium heat, stirring continuously, for 4–5 minutes until the mixture thickens and it begins to smell of caramel. (Don't have the heat too high or the condensed milk will burn.)

4 Take the pan off the heat and leave the mixture to cool for 1-2 minutes. Pour it into the biscuit case, then allow to cool completely and chill for at least 1 hour.

5 Just before serving whip the cream until it forms soft peaks. Halve the bananas lengthways, then slice them and toss them in the lemon juice. Fold two-thirds into the cream, then spoon over the toffee layer. Arrange the remaining bananas on top. Loosen the edge of the biscuit crust with a palette knife, remove the tin and transfer the pie to a serving plate. Sprinkle with grated chocolate and serve cut into wedges.

# Key
# LIME
# PIE

**AFFORDABILITY 2**

6 tablespoons unsalted butter, melted, plus extra for greasing
200 g (7 oz) digestive biscuits, crushed
4 tablespoons caster sugar
3 eggs, separated
400 g (13 oz) can full-fat condensed milk
125 ml (4 fl oz) lime juice
1 tablespoon lemon juice
2 teaspoons grated lime rind

**Topping**
250 ml (8 fl oz) double cream
1 tablespoon icing sugar
vanilla extract
lime slices, to decorate (optional)

Serves **8**
Prep time **30 minutes, plus chilling**
Cooking time **15-20 minutes**

1 Lightly grease a 23 cm (9 inch) springform cake tin with some of the unsalted butter.

2 Mix together the biscuit crumbs, butter and half the sugar and press the mixture over the bottom and up the sides of the cake tin. Refrigerate.

3 Beat the egg yolks lightly together until creamy. Add the condensed milk, lime and lemon juice and lime rind and beat until well mixed and slightly thickened. In another bowl beat the egg whites until stiff. Add the remainder of the sugar and continue beating until the meringue holds soft peaks. Use a large metal spoon to fold the meringue mixture gently but thoroughly into the lime mixture.

4 Spoon the filling into the crust and smooth the top. Bake in a preheated oven, 160°C (325°F), Gas Mark 3, for 15-20 minutes or until the filling is just firm and lightly browned on top. Cool, then refrigerate for at least 3 hours.

5 Before serving whip the cream until it begins to thicken. Add the icing sugar and vanilla extract and continue whipping until it forms thick swirls. Spread the cream over the top of the chilled pie. Decorate with twisted lime slices, if liked. Remove the side of the cake tin just before serving and serve well chilled.

# Quick
## TIRAMISU

**AFFORDABILITY 3**

1 Mix the coffee with 2 tablespoons sugar and the liqueur or brandy in a bowl. Toss the sponge fingers in the mixture and arrange in a serving dish, spooning over any excess liquid.

2 Beat together the custard, mascarpone and vanilla extract and spoon one-third over the sponge fingers. Sprinkle with the remaining sugar, then half the remaining custard. Scatter with the chocolate, then spread with the remaining custard.

3 Chill for about 1 hour until the tiramisu is set. Serve dusted with cocoa powder.

5 tablespoons strong espresso coffee
75 g (3 oz) dark muscovado sugar
4 tablespoons coffee liqueur or 3 tablespoons brandy
75 g (3 oz) sponge finger biscuits, broken into large pieces
400 g (13 oz) good-quality ready-made custard
250 g (8 oz) mascarpone cheese
1 teaspoon vanilla extract
50 g (2 oz) plain dark chocolate, finely chopped
cocoa powder, for dusting

Serves **4-6**
Prep time **15 minutes, plus chilling**

# *Spanish* CUSTARD CREAMS

THESE CREAMY CINNAMON-FLAVOURED CUSTARDS, KNOWN AS NATILLAS IN SPAIN, ARE PERFECT TO FOLLOW A SPICY MAIN COURSE. YOU CAN ADD FINELY GRATED ORANGE OR LEMON RIND TO THE MIXTURE FOR ADDED FLAVOUR IF YOU LIKE.

750 ml (1¼ pints) semi-skimmed milk
1 cinnamon stick
6 egg yolks
150 g (5 oz) golden caster sugar
2 teaspoons cornflour
ground cinnamon, for dusting
sweet biscuits, to serve (optional)

Serves **4**
Prep time **15 minutes, plus chilling**
Cooking time **10 minutes**

1 Put all but 50 ml (2 fl oz) of the milk in a saucepan, add the cinnamon stick and bring to the boil over a medium heat.

2 Meanwhile, beat the egg yolks and sugar with an electric whisk in a large bowl until light and frothy.

3 Blend the cornflour with the remaining milk and add to the egg yolk mixture. Beat well to combine.

4 When the milk comes to the boil, remove from the heat and remove the cinnamon stick. Gradually add the egg mixture, stirring constantly, and then return the pan to a low heat and cook, stirring constantly, until the custard thickens. Remove from the heat and leave to cool before spooning into individual bowls or dessert glasses.

5 Cover and chill for 2-3 hours or overnight. Lightly dust with ground cinnamon before serving with sweet biscuits, if liked.

# SUMMER
## BERRY **SORBET**

1 Put a shallow plastic container into the freezer to chill ready for the sorbet.

2 Whizz the frozen berries, cordial, Kirsch and lime juice in a food processor or blender to give a smooth purée. Take care not to over-process the purée because this will soften the mixture too much.

3 Spoon the sorbet into the chilled container and freeze for at least 25 minutes. Spoon into bowls and serve.

250 g (8 oz) frozen mixed summer berries
75 ml (3 fl oz) spiced berry cordial
2 tablespoons Kirsch
1 tablespoon lime juice

Serves **2**
Prep time **5 minutes**
Freezing time **25 minutes**

CHUNKY POTATO CHIPS

ROASTED TOMATO SAUCE

GRAVY

GLOSSY CHOCOLATE SAUCE

# BACK TO BASICS

# GRAVY

GOOD-QUALITY CUTS OF ROASTED MEAT OR POULTRY PROVIDE DELICIOUS FATS AND JUICES FOR A WELL-FLAVOURED GRAVY. AFTER ROASTING, DRAIN THE MEAT, COVER IT LOOSELY WITH KITCHEN FOIL AND MAKE THE GRAVY WHILE THE MEAT STANDS.

pan juices from roasted meat
1 tablespoon plain flour (less for a thin gravy)
300-400 ml (10-14 fl oz) liquid (this could be water, drained from the accompanying vegetables; stock; half stock and half water; or half wine and half water)
salt and pepper

Makes **about 600 ml (1 pint)**
Cooking time **5 minutes**

1 Tilt the roasting tin and skim off the fat from the surface with a large serving spoon until you are left with the pan juices and just a thin layer of fat.

2 Sprinkle the flour into the tin and stir with a wooden spoon over a moderate heat, scraping up all the residue, particularly from around the edges.

3 Gradually pour the liquid into the tin, stirring well until the gravy is thick and glossy. Let the mixture bubble, then check the seasoning, adding a little salt and pepper if necessary.

# CREAMY **BREAD** SAUCE

1 Peel the onions but leave them whole and stud them with the cloves. Put them in a saucepan with the milk and bay leaves and bring the milk almost to the boil. Reduce the heat and cook on the lowest setting for 10 minutes to let the flavours infuse the milk.

2 Remove the onions from the saucepan and add the breadcrumbs, butter, peppercorns and plenty of grated nutmeg. Cook gently for 5 minutes until the sauce is thick and pulpy.

3 Stir in the cream and season with salt and pepper to taste. Serve hot sprinkled with extra grated nutmeg, if liked.

2 onions
8 cloves
450 ml (¾ pint) full-fat milk
2 bay leaves
150 g (5 oz) fresh white breadcrumbs
25 g (1 oz) butter
1 tablespoon green peppercorns in brine, drained and lightly crushed
grated nutmeg
3 tablespoons double cream
salt

Serves **8**
Prep time **10 minutes, plus infusing**
Cooking time **15 minutes**

# BÉCHAMEL SAUCE

1 Put the milk in a saucepan with the onion, bay leaf, peppercorns and parsley stalks and bring almost to the boil. Remove the pan from the heat and leave to infuse for 20 minutes. Strain the milk through a sieve into a jug.

2 Melt the butter in a heavy-based saucepan until bubbling. Tip in the flour and stir quickly to combine. Cook the mixture gently, stirring constantly with a wooden spoon, for 1-2 minutes to make a smooth, pale roux.

3 Remove the pan from the heat and gradually whisk in the warm milk, stirring constantly until the sauce is completely smooth. Return the pan to a moderate heat and cook, stirring, until the sauce comes to the boil.

4 Reduce the heat to low and continue to cook the sauce for about 5 minutes, stirring frequently until it is smooth and glossy and thinly coats the back of the spoon. Season to taste with salt, pepper and plenty of grated nutmeg.

300 ml (½ pint) full-fat milk
½ small onion
1 bay leaf
½ teaspoon peppercorns
3-4 parsley stalks
15 g (½ oz) butter
15 g (½ oz) plain flour
pinch of grated nutmeg
salt and pepper

Serves **4**
Prep time **10 minutes, plus infusing**
Cooking time **10 minutes**

# RICH
## CHEESE
## SAUCE

300 ml (½ pint) full-fat milk
½ small onion
1 bay leaf
15 g (½ oz) butter
15 g (½ oz) plain flour
1 teaspoon green peppercorns in
  brine, rinsed and drained
75 g (3 oz) mature Cheddar
  cheese, grated
15 g (½ oz) Parmesan cheese,
  grated
pinch of grated nutmeg
salt

Serves **4**
Prep time **10 minutes**
Cooking time **10 minutes**

THIS SMOOTH, CREAMY SAUCE IS SIMPLE AND DELICIOUS AND IDEAL FOR USING UP LEFTOVER CHEESE. YOU CAN VARY THE RECIPE WITH PIECES OF GRUYERE OR STILTON OR EVEN COMBINE SEVERAL CHEESES.

1 Follow steps 1, 2 and 3 of Béchamel Sauce (see page 223) but omit the black peppercorns and parsley.

2 Lightly crush the green peppercorns in a pestle and mortar until they are broken into small pieces. Add them to the sauce with the cheeses and a little nutmeg. Cook over a gentle heat, stirring frequently, for about 5 minutes until smooth and glossy. Check the seasoning and serve hot.

# APPLE SAUCE

A CLASSIC ACCOMPANIMENT TO ROAST PORK AND GOOSE, APPLE SAUCE IS ALSO DELICIOUS WITH CHICKEN, LAMB, DUCK, GAME AND OTHER RICH, FATTY MEATS.

**1** Melt the butter in a heavy-based saucepan. Add the apples, sugar, cloves, lemon rind and juice and a small pinch of salt.

**2** Cover the pan with a lid and leave to cook gently over the lowest heat for about 20 minutes, stirring the mixture occasionally, until the apples are very soft and mushy. Check the seasoning, adding a little more lemon juice for a tangier flavour, if liked. Transfer to a sauce boat and serve warm or cold.

50 g (2 oz) unsalted butter
3 large cooking apples, peeled, cored and chopped
50 g (2 oz) caster sugar
6 whole cloves
finely grated rind and juice of 1 lemon
salt

Serves **6**
Prep time **10 minutes**
Cooking time **20 minutes**

# MINT SAUCE

THIS CLASSIC SAUCE GOES WITH PAN-FRIED DUCK BREASTS AS WELL AS GRILLED AND ROAST LAMB. DON'T THROW AWAY ANY LEFTOVER MINT SAUCE AFTER A LAMB DINNER – ADD A SPLASH OF OLIVE OIL AND SERVE IT AS A DRESSING FOR WARM NEW POTATOES OR DRIZZLE OVER PEAS OR MANGETOUT.

**1** Pull the mint leaves from their stalks and chop the leaves finely.

**2** Put the mint in a small bowl with the sugar and the boiling water. Leave to infuse for 5 minutes, stirring once or twice until the sugar dissolves.

**3** Add the vinegar and leave to stand for about 1 hour before serving.

15 g (½ oz) mint
1 tablespoon caster sugar
1 tablespoon boiling water
2 tablespoons white wine vinegar

Serves **6**
Prep time **10 minutes, plus infusing**

# SATAY
# SAUCE

THIS SAUCE IS DELICIOUSLY RICH, SPICY AND PEANUTTY AND SERVES SEVERAL
DIFFERENT PURPOSES. IT IS GENERALLY USED AS A MAIN MEAL ACCOMPANIMENT,
BUT IT'S ALSO GOOD AS A DIPPING SAUCE, SERVED ON A PLATTER WITH A SELECTION
OF VEGETABLES OR SMALL PIECES OF SKEWERED CHICKEN, PORK OR FISH.

1 lemon grass stalk
1 small onion, chopped
2 garlic cloves, chopped
1 teaspoon shrimp paste or Thai
   fish sauce (nam pla)
1 teaspoon tamarind paste
1 hot red chilli, deseeded and
   chopped
1 tablespoon light muscovado
   sugar
200 ml (7 fl oz) coconut milk
175 g (6 oz) smooth or crunchy
   peanut butter
1 tablespoon soy sauce

Serves **4-6**
Prep time **10 minutes**
Cooking time **7 minutes**

**1** Trim the ends from the lemon grass and remove any coarse or damaged outer leaves. Cut the stalk into thin slices.

**2** Put the lemon grass, onion, garlic, shrimp paste or fish sauce, tamarind paste and chilli into a food processor or blender. Add 2 tablespoons water and the sugar and blend to a paste, scraping down the mixture from the sides of the bowl with a spatula if necessary.

**3** Transfer the mixture to a saucepan with the coconut milk. Bring almost to the boil (watching closely so the coconut milk does not boil over), then reduce the heat and simmer gently for 5 minutes.

**4** Add the peanut butter and soy sauce and cook very gently for 2 minutes or until the sauce is heated through and thickened. Check the seasoning, adding a dash more soy sauce, if liked, and more coconut milk if the sauce is too thick. Transfer to a serving bowl and serve warm.

# ROASTED TOMATO SAUCE

**1** Halve the tomatoes and arrange them, cut sides up, in a large, shallow, ovenproof dish or roasting tin. Drizzle with 2 tablespoons oil, the sugar and seasoning. Roast in a preheated oven, 200°C (400°F), Gas Mark 6, for 40 minutes or until the tomatoes are soft and beginning to colour.

**2** Gently fry the onion in the remaining oil in a saucepan for about 10 minutes or until it is soft, adding the garlic for the last couple of minutes. Blend the tomatoes in a food processor or blender and add to the pan with the oregano.

**3** Cook gently for 5-10 minutes or until slightly thickened. Check the seasoning and serve.

1 kg (2 lb) very ripe tomatoes
4 tablespoons olive oil
1 teaspoon caster sugar
1 onion, finely chopped
4 garlic cloves, crushed
2 tablespoons chopped oregano
salt and pepper

Makes **750 ml (1¼ pints)**
Prep time **10 minutes**
Cooking time **50 minutes**

# PESTO

MAKING PESTO WITH A PESTLE AND MORTAR FILLS THE AIR WITH THE
WONDERFUL FRAGRANCE OF CRUSHED BASIL LEAVES BUT IS MORE TIME
CONSUMING THAN THE QUICK AND EASY FOOD PROCESSOR METHOD USED
HERE. FRESHLY MADE PESTO HAS NUMEROUS USES, MOST COMMONLY AS
A PASTA SAUCE BUT ALSO TO FLAVOUR SOUPS, STEWS AND RISOTTOS.

50 g (2 oz) basil, including stalks
50 g (2 oz) pine nuts
65 g (2½ oz) Parmesan cheese,
   grated
2 garlic cloves, chopped
125 ml (4 fl oz) olive oil
salt

Serves **4**
Prep time **5 minutes**

**1** Tear the basil into pieces and put them into a food processor
with the pine nuts, Parmesan and garlic.

**2** Blend lightly until the nuts and cheese are broken into
small pieces, scraping the mixture down from the sides of
the bowl with a spatula if necessary.

**3** Add the olive oil and a little salt and blend to a thick paste.
It can be kept, covered, in the refrigerator for up to 5 days.

# Fresh HERB BUTTER

RICH AND DELICIOUS, FLAVOURED BUTTERS MAKE SOME OF THE BEST AND SIMPLEST SAUCES AS THEY MELT OVER GRILLED, BAKED OR PAN-FRIED MEAT OR FISH. THEY'RE EASY TO MAKE, CAN BE PREPARED AHEAD AND EVEN FROZEN.

**1** Put the butter in a small bowl with the salt, parsley, chives, lemon juice and several grinds of black pepper. (Unsalted butter is best, but if you only have salted, leave out the additional salt.)

**2** Beat the mixture together with a wooden spoon until evenly combined.

**3** If you are not using the butter immediately it can be shaped into a roll and chilled for up to two days, or frozen for several weeks, a worthwhile way of using up a large quantity of fresh herbs. Simply turn the mixture on to a strip of greaseproof paper and bring the sides of the paper up over the butter, gently squeezing it into a sausage shape about 3 cm (1¼ inches) in diameter. Chill or freeze the butter until you are ready to use it. If it is frozen leave it at room temperature for 20-30 minutes before serving.

100 g (3½ oz) unsalted butter, softened
¼ teaspoon salt
2 tablespoons finely chopped parsley
2 tablespoons finely snipped chives
2 teaspoons lemon juice
pepper

Serves **4-6**
Prep time **3 minutes, plus chilling**

# CHUNKY
## POTATO CHIPS

THIS IS THE NO-FUSS VERSION OF TRADITIONAL CHIPS. THEY ARE SIMPLE TO MAKE – YOU CAN POP THEM IN THE OVEN AND FORGET ABOUT THEM (UNLIKE FRIED CHIPS) – AND ARE A GOOD ACCOMPANIMENT TO PAN-FRIED, BAKED OR GRILLED FISH.

1 kg (2 lb) baking potatoes
150 ml (¼ pint) mild olive oil or
　groundnut oil
1 teaspoon paprika
1 teaspoon celery salt
salt and pepper

Serves **4**
Prep time **10 minutes**
Cooking time **50 minutes**

**1** Cut the potatoes into 1 cm (½ inch) slices, then cut each slice into chunky chips.

**2** Brush a large roasting tin with a little of the oil and heat it in a preheated oven, 220°C (425°F), Gas Mark 7, for 5 minutes.

**3** Scatter the chips in the tin, drizzle with the remaining oil and sprinkle with the paprika and celery salt. Mix until well coated and bake for 45 minutes, turning the chips occasionally, until they are golden. Serve sprinkled with salt and pepper.

# BOILED RICE

1 Put the rice in a sieve and wash it under running warm water, rubbing the grains together between your hands to get rid of any excess starch.

2 Put the rice into a saucepan and add the stock. Set the pan on the smallest ring on the hob and bring it to the boil. Give it a quick stir then reduce the heat to a simmer. Cover with a lid and leave to cook for 15 minutes. Turn off the heat and allow the rice to steam with the lid on for another 20 minutes. Don't be tempted to lift the lid to check what's going on.

3 To serve fluff up the grains of rice with a spoon or fork.

350 g (11½ oz) Thai jasmine or long grain rice
300 ml (½ pint) Vegetable or Chicken Stock (see pages 234 and 235)

Serves **4**
Prep time **10 minutes**
Cooking time **40 minutes**

# YORKSHIRE PUDDINGS

1 To make the batter, sift the flour and salt into a large bowl and make a well in the centre. Add the milk or milk and water and beat until smooth and bubbly. Whisk the eggs in a clean bowl, then fold it quickly into the batter. Leave to stand for 30 minutes.

2 Pour ½ teaspoon oil into each of 12 deep muffin tins and place in a preheated oven, 220°C (425°F), Gas Mark 7, for 5 minutes until very hot. Quickly pour the batter into the tins to half-fill them, return them to the oven and bake for about 20 minutes until well-risen, crisp and golden brown.

125 g (4 oz) plain flour
pinch of salt
150 ml (¼ pint) milk or half milk and half water
2 eggs
oil, for greasing

Makes **12**
Prep time **10 minutes, plus standing**
Cooking time **20-25 minutes**

# OMELETTE

2 eggs
15 g (½ oz) butter
salt and pepper

Serves **1**
Prep time **2 minutes**
Cooking time **3-4 minutes**

**1** Break the eggs into a bowl and beat lightly with a balloon whisk. Whisk in 1 tablespoon water and season well with salt and pepper. Do not over-beat because this will ruin the texture of the finished omelette.

**2** Set a frying pan over a gentle heat and, when it is hot, add the butter. Tip the pan so that the entire inner surface is coated with butter. When the butter is foaming, but not browned, tip in the eggs.

**3** Leave for a few seconds then, using a spatula, draw the mixture away from the edge of the pan into the centre, allowing the eggs to run to the sides. Repeat the process twice more, by which time the eggs should have set. Cook for a further 30 seconds until the underside is golden and top still slightly runny and creamy. Tilt the pan and, with the spatula, carefully turn the omelette on to a plate, folding it in half in the process.

## Grow your own ...

... cooking herbs that is! You don't need a big garden – or any outside space for that matter – to grow some essential herbs. For the price of a few plastic containers and packets of seeds, you could have your own collection of basil, parsley and mint, ready to add another level to boring soups and sauces.

# CRUSHED MINTED **PEAS**

*A COMPULSORY ACCOMPANIMENT TO THE BEST FISH AND CHIPS, THIS IS THE HOMEMADE ANSWER TO THE PALE, SLOPPY PEA PURÉE THAT IS OFTEN SOLD TO PARTNER BOUGHT FISH AND CHIPS.*

1 Cook the peas with the mint in a large saucepan of lightly salted boiling water for about 5 minutes or until tender. Drain and return to the pan, discarding the mint.

2 Stir in the butter and crème fraîche and use a potato masher to crush the peas roughly. Season to taste with salt and pepper and reheat gently.

400 g (13 oz) peas, shelled
several sprigs of mint
25 g (1 oz) butter
2 tablespoons crème fraîche
salt and pepper

Serves **4-6**
Prep time **10 minutes**
Cooking time **5 minutes**

# **ROAST** VEGETABLE *&* **HERB** COUSCOUS

1 Put the pumpkin, courgettes and onion in a roasting tin with 2 tablespoons oil, season to taste with salt and pepper and stir to combine.

2 Roast in a preheated oven, 220°C (425°F), Gas Mark 7, for 25 minutes until all the vegetables are cooked.

3 Meanwhile, put the couscous in a heatproof bowl and pour over the water. Cover the bowl with a clean tea towel and leave to stand for 5 minutes or until the grains are swollen and all the liquid has been absorbed.

4 Fluff up the couscous with a fork, then stir in the roasted vegetables, cherry tomatoes and herbs.

5 Whisk together the remaining oil, the lemon juice and salt and pepper to taste in a small bowl and stir through the salad.

500 g (1 lb) pumpkin, peeled, deseeded and diced
4 courgettes, diced
1 red onion, cut into wedges
75 ml (3 fl oz) extra virgin olive oil
200 g (7 oz) couscous
250 ml (8 fl oz) boiling water
250 g (8 oz) cherry tomatoes, halved
2 tablespoons each chopped fresh coriander, mint and parsley
juice of 1 large lemon
salt and pepper

Serves **6**
Prep time **15 minutes, plus soaking**
Cooking time **25 minutes**

# **BEEF** STOCK

WHEN YOU BUY A PIECE OF BEEF, GET THE BONES AS WELL AND ASK THE BUTCHER TO CUT THEM INTO PIECES. FOR A RICHLY COLOURED STOCK, YOU CAN ROAST THE BONES IN A PREHEATED OVEN, 200°C (400°F), GAS MARK 6, FOR 45 MINUTES BEFOREHAND.

750 g (1½ lb) beef bones
1 large onion, unpeeled and
    quartered
1 large carrot, roughly chopped
2 celery sticks, roughly chopped
1 bouquet garni
1 teaspoon black peppercorns

Makes **about 1 litre (1¾ pints)**
Prep time **10 minutes**
Cooking time **3 hours**

1 Put the bones into a large, heavy-based saucepan with the onion, carrot, celery, bouquet garni and peppercorns. Add 1.8 litres (3 pints) cold water and bring slowly to the boil.

2 Reduce the heat and simmer the stock very gently for 3 hours, skimming the surface from time to time if necessary.

3 Strain the stock through a large sieve, preferably a conical one, and leave to cool. Don't squeeze the juice out of the vegetables or the stock will be cloudy.

4 Leave the stock to cool completely, then chill. Remove any layer of fat that might have set on the surface before use.

# **LAMB STOCK**

1 See the above recipe and simply substitute the beef bones for leftover lamb bones (roast them first for a darker stock), and simmer for just 1½ hours.

# CHICKEN **STOCK**

1 large chicken carcass, plus any
    trimmings
giblets, except the liver, if available
1 onion, quartered
1 celery stick, roughly chopped
1 bouquet garni or 3 bay leaves
1 teaspoon black peppercorns

Makes **about 1 litre (1¾ pints)**
Prep time **10 minutes**
Cooking time **1½ hours**

IDEALLY CHICKEN STOCK IS MADE USING A RAW CARCASS, BUT A COOKED CARCASS ALSO MAKES A WELL-FLAVOURED STOCK THAT MIGHT JUST BE A LITTLE CLOUDY.

1 Put the chicken carcass, giblets, onion, celery, bouquet garni and peppercorns into a large, heavy-based saucepan and add 1.8 litres (3 pints) cold water.

2 Make the stock following the recipe for Beef Stock (see above) but simmer it for just 1½ hours.

# VEGETABLE STOCK

THE VEGETABLES CAN VARY BUT MAKE SURE YOU INCLUDE SOME ONION AND OMIT VEGETABLES WITH STRONG FLAVOURS AND STARCHY ONES LIKE POTATOES. FOR A DARK STOCK, LEAVE THE SKINS ON THE ONIONS AND USE PLENTY OF MUSHROOMS.

**1** Heat the oil in a large, heavy-based saucepan and gently fry all the vegetables for 5 minutes.

**2** Add 1.5 litres (2½ pints) cold water, then follow the method for Beef Stock (see opposite), but simmering the stock for just 40 minutes.

1 tablespoon sunflower oil
2 onions, roughly chopped
2 carrots, roughly chopped
2 celery sticks, roughly chopped
500 g (1 lb) mixture of other vegetables (such as parsnips, fennel, leeks, courgettes, mushrooms and tomatoes)
1 bouquet garni
1 teaspoon black peppercorns

Makes **about 1 litre (1¾ pints)**
Prep time **10 minutes**
Cooking time **45 minutes**

# FISH STOCK

DON'T USE OILY FISH IN A STOCK — IT WILL MAKE IT GREASY AND GIVE IT AN OVERPOWERING FLAVOUR.

**1** Melt the butter in a large, heavy-based saucepan until bubbling. Add all the vegetables and fry gently for 5 minutes to soften them slightly but without browning.

**2** Add the fish bones, wine, parsley, lemon slices, peppercorns and 1 litre (1¾ pints) cold water.

**3** Follow the method for Beef Stock (see opposite), but simmering the stock for just 20 minutes.

25 g (1 oz) butter
3 shallots, roughly chopped
1 small leek, roughly chopped
1 celery stick or piece of fennel, roughly chopped
1 kg (2 lb) white fish or shellfish bones, heads and trimmings
150 ml (¼ pint) dry white wine
several parsley stalks
½ lemon, sliced
1 teaspoon black or white peppercorns

Makes **about 1 litre (1¾ pints)**
Prep time **5 minutes**
Cooking time **25 minutes**

# *Glossy*
## **CHOCOLATE** SAUCE

A GOOD CHOCOLATE SAUCE SHOULD BE SMOOTH AND GLOSSY AND TASTE ALMOST LIKE PURE MELTED CHOCOLATE. USE A GOOD QUALITY DARK CHOCOLATE WITH ABOUT 70 PER CENT COCOA SOLIDS TO GIVE A RICH FLAVOUR AND PLENTY OF SHEEN. TAKE CARE NOT TO OVERHEAT THE CHOCOLATE OR THE SAUCE WILL DEVELOP A GRAINY TEXTURE.

125 g (4 oz) caster sugar
200 g (7 oz) plain dark chocolate, chopped
25 g (1 oz) unsalted butter

Serves **5-6**
Prep time **5 minutes**
Cooking time **2-3 minutes**

1 Put the sugar in a small, heavy-based saucepan and add 125 ml (4 fl oz) water. Cook over a low heat, stirring constantly with a wooden spoon, until the sugar has dissolved.

2 Bring the syrup to the boil and boil for 1 minute, then remove the pan from the heat and leave to cool for 1 minute. Tip the chocolate into the pan.

3 Add the butter and leave until the chocolate and butter have melted, stirring frequently, until the sauce is smooth and glossy. If the last of the chocolate doesn't melt completely or you want to serve the sauce warm, return the pan briefly to the lowest heat setting.

# Custard

SMOOTH, CREAMY AND COMFORTING, CUSTARD IS ALWAYS A GREAT FAVOURITE AND WELL WORTH THE EFFORT OF MAKING FROM SCRATCH.

**1** Put the vanilla pod into a heavy-based saucepan with the milk and cream and bring slowly to the boil. Remove from the heat and leave to infuse for 15 minutes.

**2** Whisk together the egg yolks and sugar in a bowl with a balloon whisk until thick and pale. Lift the vanilla pod out of the pan and scrape the seeds into the pan.

**3** Pour the milk over the creamed mixture, whisking well. Return the mixture to a clean pan and cook over a medium heat, stirring constantly with a wooden spoon, until the sauce thickly coats the back of the spoon. This will take about 5-10 minutes, but don't be tempted to increase the heat or the custard might curdle. Serve warm.

1 vanilla pod, split lengthways
300 ml (½ pint) full cream milk
300 ml (½ pint) single cream
6 egg yolks
25 g (1 oz) caster sugar

Serves **6**
Prep time **10 minutes, plus infusing**
Cooking time **10-15 minutes**

# THE BAR

MOJITO

COSMOPOLITAN

MARGARITA

MULLED WINE

BLOODY MARY

# **BLOODY** MARY

THE LEGENDARY FERNAND PETOIT, OF THE FAMOUS HARRY'S BAR IN PARIS, WAS
THE INVENTOR OF THE BLOODY MARY.

ice cubes
2 measures vodka
1 dash lemon juice
Worcestershire sauce, to taste
tomato juice, to top up
½ teaspoon cayenne pepper
salt and pepper
tomato and celery stalks, to
  decorate

**1** Put some ice cubes into a highball glass.

**2** Pour over the vodka and lemon juice, add Worcestershire
sauce to taste and top up with tomato juice. Add the
cayenne pepper and season to taste with salt and pepper. Stir to
chill. Decorate with a tomato and celery stalks and serve.

Serves **1**
Prep time **2 minutes**

# BAY
# *Breeze*

THIS IS A VARIATION OF THE CLASSIC SEA BREEZE (SEE OPPOSITE). HERE,
PINEAPPLE JUICE IS USED TO ADD A TOUCH OF SWEETNESS THAT CONTRASTS
WITH THE PIQUANT FLAVOUR OF CRANBERRIES.

ice cubes
4 measures cranberry juice
2 measures vodka
2 measures pineapple juice
lime wedges, to decorate

**1** Fill a highball glass with ice cubes and pour over the
cranberry juice.

**2** Pour the vodka and pineapple juice into a chilled
cocktail shaker, shake well and gently pour over the
cranberry juice and ice in the glass. Decorate with lime
wedges and serve with long straws.

Serves **1**
Prep time **2 minutes**

# SEA BREEZE

THIS REFRESHING CONTEMPORARY CLASSIC IS THE TANGIER SISTER DRINK TO BAY BREEZE, MADE WITH PINK GRAPEFRUIT RATHER THAN PINEAPPLE JUICE.

1 Put some ice cubes into a highball or hurricane glass.

2 Pour over the vodka and fruit juices. Squeeze the lime wedges into the drink and stir lightly before serving.

ice cubes
2 measures vodka
4 measures cranberry juice
2 measures pink grapefruit
  juice
2 lime wedges

Serves **1**
Prep time **2 minutes**

## Shaking

Shaking is used to mix ingredients quickly and thoroughly and to chill the drink before serving.

Half-fill the cocktail shaker or the Boston glass (if using a Boston shaker) with ice cubes (or the amount specified in the recipe) or add cracked or crushed ice. If the recipe calls for a chilled glass, add a few ice cubes and some water to the glass and swirl them around before discarding. Add the remaining ingredients to the shaker. Put on the strainer and cap or, if using a Boston shaker, place the shaking tin over the glass. Shake until condensation forms on the outside of the shaker. Use both hands to hold either end of the shaker and to prevent it from slipping from your grip. The cocktail is then ready to be strained into the glass for serving by removing the cap but keeping the strainer in place.

# MOSCOW MULE

THIS WAS INVENTED IN 1941 BY AN EMPLOYEE OF A US DRINKS FIRM IN CONJUNCTION WITH A LOS ANGELES BAR OWNER WHO WAS OVERSTOCKED WITH GINGER BEER.

1 Put the cracked ice into a cocktail shaker. Add the vodka and lime juice and shake until a frost forms on the outside of the shaker.

2 Pour, without straining, into a highball glass, top up with ginger beer and stir lightly. Decorate with lime or orange wheels and serve.

3-4 ice cubes, cracked
2 measures vodka
juice of 2 limes
ginger beer, to top up
lime or orange wheels, to
  decorate

Serves **1**
Prep time **2 minutes**

# BLACK RUSSIAN

THIS IS THE ORIGINAL COCKTAIL, DATING BACK TO THE 1950s. NOWADAYS, IT IS OFTEN SERVED AS A LONG DRINK, TOPPED UP WITH CHILLED COLA.

4-6 ice cubes, cracked
2 measures vodka
1 measure Kahlúa
chocolate stick, to decorate
  (optional)

Serves **1**
Prep time **2 minutes**

 1 Put the cracked ice into a rocks (old-fashioned) glass. Pour over the vodka and Kahlúa and stir.

2 Decorate with a chocolate stick, if you like, and serve.

# WHITE RUSSIAN

THIS MODERN TAKE ON THE BLACK RUSSIAN USES TIA MARIA AND CREAM TO GIVE THE DRINK ITS DISTINCTIVE COLOUR AND TEXTURE.

6 ice cubes, cracked
1 measure vodka
1 measure Tia Maria
1 measure full-fat milk or double
  cream

Serves **1**
Prep time **2 minutes**

1 Put half the cracked ice into a cocktail shaker and put the remaining cracked ice into a highball glass.

2 Add all the remaining ingredients to the shaker and shake until a frost forms on the outside of the shaker. Strain over the ice in the glass. Serve with a straw.

## Muddling

This is the technique used to bring out the flavours of fruit and herbs using a blunt tool called a muddler. A famous example is the Mojito, where mint, sugar syrup and lime wedges are muddled in the bottom of a highball glass before the remaining ingredients are added.

Remove the mint leaves from their stems and put them into the bottom of a highball glass. Add the sugar syrup and lime wedges. Hold the glass firmly with one hand and use the muddler to press down on the mint and lime wedges. Twist the muddler and press firmly to release the flavour of the mint and to break it down with the juice from the lime wedges. Continue this process for about 30 seconds, then top up the glass with crushed ice. Add the remaining ingredients to the glass, as specified in the recipe

# MOJITO

THIS IS A COOLING, EFFERVESCENT COCKTAIL BORN
– THANKS TO PROHIBITION – AMID CUBA'S THRIVING
INTERNATIONAL BAR CULTURE. IT PROBABLY
DERIVED FROM THE MINT JULEP.

12 mint leaves, plus an extra
  sprig to decorate
½ measure sugar syrup (see
  page 245)
4 lime wedges
crushed ice
2 measures white rum
soda water, to top up

1 Put the mint, sugar syrup and lime wedges into a highball
  glass and muddle together (see left).

2 Fill the glass with crushed ice, pour over the rum and stir.
  Top up with soda water. Decorate with a mint sprig and
serve with straws.

Serves **1**
Prep time **2 minutes**

# *Rusty* NAIL

AN AFTER-DINNER DRINK WHOSE NAME IS PROBABLY DUE TO ITS COLOUR RATHER
THAN IMMIGRANT SCOTTISH BARTENDERS STIRRING THE COCKTAIL WITH A RUSTY
NAIL BEFORE SERVING IT TO THEIR AMERICAN PATRONS, AS LEGEND HAS IT.

1 Fill a rocks (old-fashioned) glass with ice cubes.

ice cubes
1½ measures Scotch whisky
1 measure Drambuie

2 Pour over the whisky and Drambuie and serve.

Serves **1**
Prep time **2 minutes**

# DRY MARTINI

THE MOST FAMOUS COCKTAIL OF ALL WAS INVENTED AT THE KNICKERBOCKER HOTEL IN NEW YORK IN 1910. LEMON RIND IS SOMETIMES USED AS A DECORATION INSTEAD OF A GREEN OLIVE.

5-6 ice cubes
½ measure dry vermouth
3 measures gin
green olive, to decorate

Serves **1**
Prep time **2 minutes**

1 Put the ice cubes into a mixing glass. Pour over the vermouth and gin and stir (never shake) vigorously and evenly without splashing.

2 Strain into a chilled Martini (cocktail) glass. Decorate with a green olive and serve.

# COSMOPOLITAN

MANY PEOPLE LAY CLAIM TO BEING THE INVENTOR OF THE COSMOPOLITAN; HOWEVER, IT IS A RELATIVELY RECENT COCKTAIL THAT HAS BECOME SOMETHING OF A CLASSIC ALREADY.

1 Put the cracked ice into a cocktail shaker. Add all the remaining ingredients and shake until a frost forms on the outside of the shaker.

2 Strain into a chilled Martini (cocktail) glass. Decorate with an orange rind twist and serve.

6 ice cubes, cracked
1 measure vodka
½ measure Cointreau
1 measure cranberry juice
juice of ½ lime
orange rind twist, to decorate

Serves **1**
Prep time **2 minutes**

## Stirring

'Shaken or stirred?' is the usual response from a bartender when a Martini is ordered and, despite James Bond's famously declared preference, Martinis are best served stirred, not shaken. A cocktail is prepared by stirring when it must maintain clarity yet also requires the ingredients to be mixed and chilled. This ensures that there is no fragmented ice or air bubbles throughout the drink. Some stirred cocktails will require the ingredients to be prepared in a mixing glass, then strained into the serving glass with a fine strainer, while others call for the drink to be prepared and stirred in the same glass.

Add the ingredients, in the order stated in the recipe, either to the mixing glass or the serving glass. Using a bar spoon, either lightly or vigorously stir the drink, again according to the recipe. It is important to follow the recipe exactly because some drinks will require just a slight blending of the ingredients and will not benefit from over-stirring. Finish the drink with any decoration required and serve.

## Sugar syrup

This is used as a sweetener in lots of cocktails. It blends into a cold drink more quickly than sugar and adds body. You can buy it in bottles, but it's very easy to make your own. Simply bring equal quantities of caster sugar and water to the boil in a small saucepan, stirring continuously, then boil for 1–2 minutes without stirring. Sugar syrup can be kept in a sterilized bottle in the refrigerator for up to two months.

# HANGOVERS &
# DRINKING
# GAMES

With a bottle of gin, a bottle of vodka and a few choice mixers, you can rustle up a whole selection of chic-sounding cocktails and transform a dull Friday night into a swish soirée. Add some nibbles and a couple of drinking games and you've got yourself a real party.

## DRINK AND THINK

Whoever starts has to call out the name of someone famous. The next in the line, or circle, must use the first letter of the last name called out for the first name of their famous person – for example, Elvis Presley could be followed by Paul McCartney and so on.

## SHOT ROULETTE

This is pretty self-explanatory. Gather together as many shot glasses as there are guests and fill them all with water, except one, which you fill with a vodka shot. Pass them around and whoever downs the vodka sits out the next round. Keep going until you have a winner.

## THE MORNING AFTER

Whilst we advise you to drink in moderation, pace yourself and know when it's time to go home, we know that over-indulgence can be a part of many students' lives. So, instead of going on about memory loss and the sudden desire to eat kebabs, we're here to pick up the pieces and offer some essential advice for the morning after.

## A WALK IN THE PARK

While a lie-in is the usual way to combat a thumping head, it is more beneficial to drag yourself out of bed. Fresh air and exercise will help to rid your body of the alcohol. And, if there's a café at the end of that walk, with free tea refills, so much the better.

## EAT YOUR WAY TO SOBRIETY

There's a reason why people have greasy fry-ups: the fat, salt and carbohydrates help to speed up the recovery process. But don't forget to drink plenty of water as well.

## THINK AHEAD

It's always best to tackle a hangover before it's arrived.

- Drink a large glass of water before bed.
- Try to eat something. A piece of toast, banana or biscuit are easy, even with blurred vision.
- Take a drink up to bed with you (non-alcoholic that is), so you can top up on fluids during the night.

# WHISKY MAC

A WARMING SLUG MADE WITH EQUAL MEASURES OF SCOTCH AND GINGER WINE, THIS IS A DELICIOUS WINTER PICK-ME-UP.

3-4 ice cubes
1 measure Scotch whisky
1 measure ginger wine

Serves **1**
Prep time **2 minutes**

1 Put the ice cubes into a rocks (old-fashioned) glass.

2 Pour over the whisky and ginger wine, stir lightly and serve.

# MARGARITA

THE EXACT ORIGIN OF THIS FAMOUS DRINK IS UNKNOWN. ONE STORY TELLS OF A SHOWGIRL WHO WAS ALLERGIC TO ALL ALCOHOL EXCEPT TEQUILA. SHE ASKED A BARTENDER TO CREATE HER A COCKTAIL WITH THE SPIRIT AND THE REST IS HISTORY.

1 lime wedge
rock salt
ice cubes
2 measures Tequila
1 measure lime juice
1 measure triple sec
lime wheel, to decorate

Serves **1**
Prep time **2 minutes**

1 Moisten the rim of a Margarita (coupette) glass with the lime wedge and frost with the salt (see right).

2 Half-fill a cocktail shaker with ice cubes. Add all the remaining ingredients and shake until a frost forms on the outside of the shaker. Strain into the glass. Decorate with a lime wheel and serve.

## Frosting glasses

Although not strictly a decoration, this effect does add to the final look of a drink. As with some other decorations, frosting can either perform a practical function, as in the Margarita, or a purely visual one. In general, glasses are either frosted with sugar or salt, but more unusual frostings can be used to complement flavours in cocktails, such as cocoa powder with a chocolate cocktail.

Dip the rim of the glass in a small saucer of lime or lemon juice, lightly beaten egg white or water. Spread the desired frosting on a clean work surface or on a small plate or saucer. Place the glass on the frosting, twisting slightly to ensure you get an even coating. Clean excess frosting from the inside of the glass using a lemon or lime wedge to prevent it from contaminating the cocktail.

# SANGRIA

THIS CLASSIC SPANISH PUNCH USES RED WINE AS ITS FOUNDATION. WITH THE ADDITION OF CHOPPED FRUIT AND CINNAMON, IT'S LIKE A SUMMERTIME VERSION OF MULLED WINE.

1 Put some ice cubes into a large jug. Add the wine, brandy, fruit wedges and one cinnamon stick and stir well.

2 When ready to serve, top up with the chilled lemonade and stir. Serve in glasses decorated with orange, lemon and apple wheels and cinnamon sticks.

ice cubes
2 bottles light Spanish red wine, chilled
5 measures brandy
orange, lemon and apple wedges, plus orange, lemon and apple wheels
cinnamon sticks
about 450 ml (¾ pint) lemonade, chilled

Serves **10-12**
Prep time **5 minutes**

# MULLED WINE

1 Pour the wine, apple juice, 300 ml (½ pint) water and orange juice into a large, heavy-based saucepan.

2 Add the sliced orange and lemon, the cinnamon stick, cloves and bay leaves, then mix in the sugar and brandy. Heat, stirring, until the sugar has dissolved, then bring to the boil and simmer gently for 10 minutes.

3 Keep warm over a low heat and ladle into heatproof glasses to serve.

750 ml (1¼ pints) or 1 bottle inexpensive red wine
300 ml (½ pint) clear apple juice
juice of 1 orange
1 orange, sliced
½ lemon, sliced
1 cinnamon stick, halved
6 cloves
2 bay leaves
125 g (4 oz) caster sugar
150 ml (1¼ pint) brandy

Serves **6**
Prep time **5 minutes**
Cooking time **10-15 minutes**

# B-52

THIS IS THE CLASSIC LAYERED SHOT THAT TASTES JUST AS GOOD AS IT LOOKS, WITH A WONDERFUL WARM, SWEET FLAVOUR.

½ measure Kahlúa
½ measure Baileys Irish Cream
½ measure Grand Marnier

Serves **1**
Prep time **3 minutes**

1 Using a bar spoon, carefully layer the three ingredients, in order, in a shot glass (see below).

2 Serve immediately.

## Layering

This is also referred to as pousse café. The technique involves a number of spirits and liqueurs being carefully layered, one by one, in a shot glass, and the drink is then consumed in one mouthful. It is achieved by using the flat end of a bar spoon against the surface of each liquid and works because liquids have different densities, so some will be lighter than others and will therefore float on the layers beneath.

Pour the first liquid ingredient listed in the recipe into the shot glass, being careful not to allow any on the side of the glass. Position the bar spoon in the centre of the glass with the rounded part of the spoon facing towards you. The spoon should be resting against the inside of the glass while also being in contact with the first liquid ingredient. Carefully and slowly pour the second liquid ingredient down the bar spoon so that it flows into the glass along the spoon and sits on top of the first liquid, creating a second layer. Repeat with the third ingredient, then carefully remove the bar spoon.

# PIMM'S COCKTAIL

THIS IS MORE ALCOHOLIC THAN THE ORIGINAL, WITH THE ADDITION OF GIN, BUT IT'S JUST AS REFRESHING. GINGER ALE ADDS A DELICIOUS SPICINESS TO THE DRINK.

1 Fill a highball glass with ice cubes. Build all the remaining ingredients, one by one in order, over the ice.

2 Decorate with cucumber strips, blueberries and orange wheels and serve.

ice cubes
1 measure Pimm's No 1
1 measure gin
2 measures lemonade
2 measures ginger ale
cucumber strips, blueberries and orange wheels, to decorate

Serves **1**
Prep time **3 minutes**

# ICED **LEMON** & MINT VODKA

1 Pour the lemon juice, cordial and vodka into a cocktail shaker and shake well.

2 Pour the cocktail into six tall glasses half-filled with ice cubes. Add a few mint sprigs and top up with tonic water. Serve immediately.

4 tablespoons lemon juice
8 tablespoons lemon cordial
125 ml (4 fl oz) vodka, chilled
ice cubes
a few mint sprigs
tonic water

Serves **6**
Prep time **6 minutes**

# INDEX

# ACKNOWLEDGEMENTS

**Picture Credits**
Key: a above, b below, c centre, l left, r right.

Octopus Publishing Group 138, 148, 211;
Stephen Conroy 18, 21, 24, 26, 29, 31, 34, 47, 63,
67, 77, 78, 79, 83, 88, 91, 104, 118, 119, 121, 127
left, 136, 141, 150, 191, 222, 224, 226, 227, 228,
229, 230, 236, 243, 245, 246; Will Heap 25, 58,
68, 127 right, 128, 130, 131, 142, 180, 189, 201,
203, 213, 215; David Jordan 49; William
Lingwood 10, 30, 86, 178, 183; David Loftus 37,
61, 206, 211, 237; Jason Lowe 43, 51, 55, 71, 112,
158, 161, 167, 168, 218; David Munns 16, 120, 132;
Sean Myers 117; Peter Myers 45; Emma Neish
56, 107, 108, 157, 169, 171; Lis Parsons 17, 20, 23,
27, 32, 33, 64, 65, 111; William Reavell 12, 19, 66,
99, 100, 154, 172, 173, 174, 175, 182, 187, 188,
208; Gareth Sambidge 96, 196, 197; William
Shaw 15; Simon Smith 13; Ian Wallace 50, 53,
57, 59, 82, 93, 94, 122, 125, 137, 143, 144, 179,
194, 198, 216; Philip Webb 41
**Shutterstock** 38br, 42br, 74br, 87br, 92ar,
98br, 113c, 124br, 134br, 151bc, 163bl, 185br,
212bc, 219ac
Additional background images: **Thinkstock**

**Publisher** Sarah Ford
**Editor** Pauline Bache
**Features Writer** Cara Frost-Sharratt
**Designer** Eoghan O'Brien
**Layout Design** Jaz Bahra and Hugh Schermuly
**Cover Design** Jo Bell
**Picture Library Manager** Jennifer Veall
**Assistant Production Manager** Caroline Alberti